Neurological Intelligence®
Volume 2

NEUROLOGICAL INTELLIGENCE®

VOLUME 2

Strategies *and* Tools
to Heal *and* Grow

Glenn S. Cohen

Library of Congress Control Number: 2023913917
Paperback ISBN: 979-8-9876567-3-0
eBook ISBN: 979-8-9876567-4-7
Audiobook ISBN: 979-8-9876567-5-4

Design by Christina Thiele, CreateForGood
Editorial production by KN Literary

CENTER
for
NEUROLOGICAL
INTELLIGENCE®
❖

You may find additional resources at www.centerforni.com

Contents

Introduction

Most of the important things in the world
have been accomplished
by people who have kept on trying
when there seemed to be no hope at all.

–Dale Carnegie

The true hero's journey begins within. This is something I've continually reminded myself of over the past twenty years of my own personal-development saga. My learning, stretching, healing, and growth did not happen overnight. There wasn't a loud trumpet announcing my arrival to empowerment and enlightenment—and I expect that kind of reception may never happen! This amazing adventure I call the living laboratory of life is an ongoing process of challenges that present us with opportunities for our learning and growth—but we ultimately have to make the choice to move in that direction.

In 2003, I began my mission to discover why I'd made so many choices that kept me stuck in a repetitive loop of negativity, obstruction, turmoil, and conflict—a loop that had begun in childhood and stalked me like a shadow into my adult life. I read book after book; I searched for the answers through acquiring knowledge I could understand logically, but all the while, I hadn't unlocked the secret that lay within me. I was still in my head and had not connected with my body to listen to or hear the wisdom of my inner voice.

Countless times, I experienced a knowingness of a choice—a choice that could take me toward greater happiness and peace. But instead of listening and responding to the voice that was telling me where to go, I remained on autopilot and stayed in the comfort zone of my disempowered (red) patterns. I continued making choices that validated my old, disempowered story and recycled the fear, shame, and pain I had become all too familiar with. I kept repeating, reenacting, and reinforcing painful emotions and self-limiting beliefs that kept me from growing into my next highest version.

As I look back over the last twenty years, I view this incredible journey as occurring in many phases, most of them nonlinear; that is, I took a few steps forward and then—*BAM!*—I made choices that set me a few steps back. Of course, at the time, I was not fully aware these challenges were blessings in disguise, as they contained my greatest learning opportunities.

I consider the summer of 2008 the beginning of the next phase of my journey. After my disability ran out from my spinal surgery in 2005, I went back into my old career as a floating pharmacist. During this time, I learned from more than 400 audiobooks that covered every healing modality I could find. I reserved one or two days a week to see my coaching clients, which numbered five to eight a week. By the summer of 2014, I finally broke through the glass ceiling of ten per week and left pharmacy for good on Labor Day weekend.

The next phase, which lasted for several years, began that weekend of 2014. I now had time to attend in-person workshops, retreats, and trainings. I also had time to watch webinars and order DVDs of lectures and workshops. At the beginning of this phase, I found myself in another chaotic relationship that inspired me to focus my efforts on truly finding a way to heal myself. It was during my self-imposed "personal-development PhD" that I slowly began to apply the knowledge I'd accumulated in my head and understand that true healing happens in the unlimited, unconscious mind that exists within the body.

Even in this phase, I was still making some choices that whacked me over the head to get me to wake up and show up! The difference at this point was I was able to search for a new approach and continue to challenge myself to go deeper and deeper into my own inner world.

Today, I have two eight-by-six-foot whiteboards on the wall in my office. I put them up in 2015, and as I kept facing challenges and learning something new, I would adjust, change, or rearrange the flow of the words on the boards until they made sense to me and my clients. In July 2020, my inner voice spoke clearly to me and said that, after eighteen years, it was time to begin writing so that I could share my mission of combining the best of the best with my own ideas, based on my personal and professional experiences. I spent millions of hours studying, combining, and molding the best of the best, which eventually became the modality I developed, which I call Neurological Intelligence (abbreviated to NI throughout this book). This is when I began writing the three volumes of my life's work. You've likely read the first (and if not, I suggest you do so!), and you now have the second in your hands.

I share this global view of my journey to help you understand that healing and growth is not a one-and-done deal. It is a never-ending series of opportunities that extend to us the choice to mindfully continue our healing and growth.

Volume 1 contains all the knowledge to help you understand how your nervous system was programmed in the past and how you continue that process moment to moment in the present. As you flowed through volume 1, you completed exercises that gave you valuable insight into how your inner world was formed and how it functions today. This information will be invaluable as you take the next steps on your journey with volume 2.

My wish is that volume 2 leads you to acquire the insights, strategies, tools, and techniques to continue your adventure. As I shared in my story, the vast amount of knowledge I gained was only the beginning. It was the foundation of making sense of how I became neurologically wounded in childhood and how I perpetuated those patterns in my adult life. It was not until I participated in experiential processes that challenged me to the core that my true healing and growth began.

Even as I write this, I am still learning, stretching, healing, and growing. I wrote volume 2 to facilitate greater smoothness in your own journey as you become the mindful manager of your meaning-machine mind.

The Goals of This Book:
The Journey Always Begins Within

Volume 1 of *Neurological Intelligence* is designed for anyone who desires to understand the science and sense behind this modality. It gives you the knowledge you will need to experience the greatest success and results with volume 2, which is for anyone who's inspired to dig deep and begin to do their inner work. After all, we have to understand how our system works before we can start applying the strategies, tools, and techniques to work our system and get to our desired outcome.

If you can answer yes to any of the following questions, you're in the right place—and this book will facilitate your journey toward tapping into the next higher version of yourself.

- Are you sick and tired of feeling sad, lost, stuck, and confused—or angry, resentful, reactive, and regretful about yourself, others, and your life?
- Are you ready to end the suffering you have been experiencing, which has been going on for far too long?
- Do you want to stop allowing the neurological wounding from your past to adversely impact the opportunities and choices you have in your present?
- Would you like to break the repeating cycle of negativity, obstruction, turmoil, and conflict within you and your committed love relationship? (If you are not in a committed

love relationship, are you ready to do the necessary healing work that will aid you in communicating more clearly and lovingly with a potential partner?)

- Are you ready to step into a process of healing, accepting, and forgiveness, in order to move forward after a difficult life transition or a heartbreaking loss?
- Would you like to transform your disempowered patterns of thoughts, emotions, behaviors, and stories (what I call TEBS) so they serve you instead of causing you to suffer?
- Would you like to end your dysfunctional family legacy patterns so you do not unconsciously and inadvertently pass them down to your children?
- Have you had enough of the same ol', same ol'—and are you willing to be uncomfortable with uncertainty to do whatever it takes to learn, stretch, heal, and grow?
- Are you ready to take absolute personal responsibility and commit to doing the work to understand and mindfully manage your inner world?

Throughout this book, you'll be urged to identify what you really want out of life—as well as which inner blocks have obstructed the way to fulfillment. Defining moments are a wake-up call for us to look for the gifts that come from our biggest challenges. When we face our biggest challenges, we have a choice to surrender to the truth by accepting that it is what it is, we are where we are, and what we have been doing is definitely *not* working. We have a choice to continue to regress into our personal abyss, go sideways doing the same thing over and over again, or do our inner work and evolve. How we perceive and receive the following statements will determine our choices. Do you choose to:

- deflect, defend, and debate—or accept, own, and change
- bury your head in the sand and keep repeating your dysfunctional patterns—or show up and do your inner work to learn, stretch, heal, and grow

No healing path is linear, and you may find yourself bouncing back and forth between empowered and disempowered patterns. The strategies, tools, and techniques in this book are meant to help interrupt this ping-pong process so that you are more consistently choosing empowered patterns. The process to gain NI is an ongoing journey of personal and relationship education, exploration, and experientials that will lead you toward achieving the outcomes you desire. It begins with an awareness and realization that every impactful neurological experience (INE) from childbirth to today is your golden opportunity to evolve in the present so you can inspire and contribute to others in the future.

Personal evolution is about having the confidence and inner strength to use the NI strategies, tools, and techniques to step out of your comfort zone as you press against the resistance of your familiar disempowered patterns. Personal evolution is also about:

- having the courage to be honest, authentic, vulnerable, open, and real (what I like to call HAVOR) about your TEBS with respect to yourself and others;
- showing love and acceptance toward all aspects of yourself, especially your wonderfully unique and special brand of weirdness;
- having empathy and compassion for your wounded inner ones, your personalities of offensive and defensive strategies (PODS), and your perfectly imperfect self;
- giving yourself permission to allow your old, repetitive, red-disempowered stories from the past to be inaccurate, incomplete, or incorrect;
- doing your inner work nonjudgmentally to reveal, release, and resolve the painful emotions from the past that get triggered in your life in the present; and
- being mindful enough to stop arguing for your limitations and, with loving kindness, change any self-limiting disempowered beliefs you use to evaluate your present experiences.

Know that as you flow through the work and processes of NI, there may be times when you feel drained or tired. You're processing a lot, so this is normal; be kind and compassionate with yourself as you go through your amazing journey.

Just remember that wounding happens from the top down, and healing occurs from the bottom up. In order to transfer and transform patterns and reveal, release, and resolve the unresolved, you need to go downstairs into your body and allow your unconscious mind to do what it needs to do without too much left-brain interference. Healing your fractured inner world cannot be achieved with left-brain analyzing, logicizing, rationalizing, and strategizing!

Here's the deal. The magnificent left brain is wonderful when we need to make sense of something or create a plan of action. The problem is our unlimited unconscious mind is not analytical, logical, rational, or strategic; it has no concept of space or time and does not know the difference between real, remembered, or imagined. When we get triggered, the elements of our unresolved memories are retrieved outside of our conscious awareness. So of course, when our thoughts, emotions, body sensations, and beliefs perceive the triggering moment through the lens of the present content and not the context of the unresolved past, it makes no sense—and cannot be analyzed, logicized, or rationalized. Through the neurological instruments you'll learn about in this book—which will create a rich inner experience in which you can see, hear, feel, or sense the unresolved past by bypassing the constraints of the left brain—you will begin to create the changes you desire. You'll continue that journey in the Re-Claiming Process, which takes you deeper into actualizing your MEL (mindful empowered leader) and healing what remains unresolved; you'll get an introduction to the first three steps of that process in section 3, and, should you choose to continue, you'll partake of the remaining steps with me in a variety of workshop formats.

So, are you ready to engage in a process to heal whatever remains unresolved in your inner world and stop the negative patterns you have been experiencing in your relationships with others and yourself?

Are you ready to learn a new, empowered way to live your life? Are you ready to show up and step up your efforts to achieve your hopes, dreams, and goals? This is your time, here, right now. Let's begin!

The Re-Claiming Process: Your Journey of Healing and Growth

In volume 1, you gained the foundational knowledge and science of NI—what I also refer to as the Re-Claiming Journey. This is akin to going to medical school and studying all there is to know about the human system. You learned about the four neurological cycles that influence the formation and functioning of your nervous system. You began exploring the three aspects of your inner world, discovered your unresolved wounds and what you would like to heal, and explored the person you would like to grow into as you move forward. Hopefully, you intentionally used your **t**ime, **e**nergy, and **a**ttention (TEA), which are some of your most important resources, especially when you mindfully harness them, to complete all the exercises and apply them to your life. And now you have an awareness of the impact that your unresolved memories, which contain your painful emotions and disempowered beliefs, had and continue to have on your inner world. After all, knowledge isn't power—it's the application of that knowledge that is truly powerful.

In this book, you will continue your journey to acquire the knowledge, strategies, tools, and techniques to begin to heal your unresolved wounds, grow into the next highest version of yourself, and become the MEL of your inner world. This will include learning about vital neurological instruments (covered in sections 1 and 2) that you'll then use to perform "inner-world surgery" on yourself—or what I call the Re-Claiming Process (covered in section 3). Think of this as your residency program. The neurological instruments form the foundation for the strategies, tools, and techniques needed to perform successful surgery on yourself.

Altogether, this book guides you through working with the two cycles that impact and infect your inner and outer worlds.

The first involves the Triggered Protective Cycle (which we cover in section 2). The objective of working with the Triggered Protective Cycle is to *recognize* and *interrupt* disempowered patterns, and then to *install with repetition* new empowered patterns. When this cycle is activated, your PODS hijack your inner world and you lose access to your MEL, and you become reactive and make choices that dishonor your true self, leaving others to feel baffled by the way you show up. These are also the patterns your committed love partner dislikes and complains about. These are the patterns that hold you back, sabotage your journey, and validate your disempowered beliefs and identity. What you are about to learn can become a lifelong prescription of personal power that will serve you well so that your inner world maintains and sustains a state that is flexible, healthy, and functional.

The second involves the Core Identity Cycle (which we cover in section 3 as we get into the Re-Claiming Process). The objective of working with the Core Identity Cycle is to *reveal*, *release*, and *resolve* your unresolved NUBs (**n**eurological **u**nresolved **b**undles)—the vulnerable, wounded aspects of self. This cycle is the fuel that influences your Triggered Protective Cycle.

Let's go through the outline of this book:

- *Section 1—NI Lab Time: Practice and Become Proficient to Give Yourself the Best Chance for Success* will introduce you to the eleven neurological instruments that form the foundation for you to effectively use the strategies and tools in this book. You will learn and practice the anchors of awareness, which include twenty-one mindfulness strategies and twenty-one VAKing (**v**isual, **a**uditory, and **k**inesthetic) tools you can select from whenever you want to recognize and interrupt your disempowered patterns. You'll have the opportunity to complete exercises for each of the strategies and tools so you understand when to pull them out of your neurological toolbox. If you were to stop reading after section 1, you'd have a number of actionable tools to keep you busy for a lifetime, but believe it or not, this is just the beginning!

- *Section 2—Busting the Boundaries of Your Triggered Protective Cycle* will teach you about "stimulus, gap, choice," which is the foundational concept that many of the processes in this book are built on. You will then study and practice the M&M technique to monitor and modify reactive patterns. The M&M technique is the strategy you will use to change your choice from one that is disempowered and reactive to one that is empowered and responsive. You'll also have the opportunity to work through recent challenges and triggers so you can apply this technique to your life and repeatedly install new, empowered patterns. Again, you can spend a lifetime practicing the M&M technique (and I hope you do!), but it's also preparation for the journey ahead, should you choose to take it.

- *Section 3—Reveal, Release, and Resolve Your Core Identity Cycle* explains the nine steps of the Re-Claiming Process. This section consists of exercises and guided meditations, which enable you to journey into your inner world so you can apply the instruments to perform inner-world surgery on yourself. Step 1 of the Re-Claiming Process is included in this book and contains three exercises you will work through to prepare you for the journeys you'll embark on. I highly suggest that you follow the directions and complete the exercises before you begin step 2. This step starts with learning about and going through strategic intentional meditative experiences (SIMEs), which will serve as the vehicle for your journey. This is the operating space you will strive to stay in that will give you the best chance of success. You will begin step 2 in this book by learning about the concepts and tools needed to guide you on your journey. For the rest of steps 2 and 3, there are QR codes with a URL that will lead you into the experiential aspects of these steps, where you can practice the demonstrations, inductions, and meditations. One thing to remember is that SIMEs are experiential processes that happen inside you. *You cannot read an experiential; you have to experience it.* With that said, it is necessary for you to access steps 4 through 9 in a live experiential format. You may choose to do this via the following options: one-on-one coaching for individualized experiences with me or a certified NI life coach; group weekend in-person workshops around the country; or weekly group workshops via Zoom, nationally or internationally. Additionally, I will be offering coach training programs for anyone who desires to become a certified neurological life coach in the NI modality. In the trainings, you will practice and experience all the steps of the Re-Claiming Process.

Using all the neurological instruments, you'll have the ability to impact the coding for the software of your inner computer so your patterns work for you instead of against you. You cannot change the content of what happened *to* you, but you can change the context—what happened *within* you. But in order to let go of the past, you have to allow yourself to let go of the present. That's your gift to yourself!

Let me explain: Most of the time, when people say they're living in the moment, that's not true—what they're living in is the left brain, which they use to make sense of the moment and judge what is happening. They're better at doing than at being. This means they cannot drop down into their bodies and work with the instruments that allow the unconscious mind to reveal, release, and resolve what remains unresolved.

In volume 1, I mentioned a story from Debbie Ford about how the challenges and struggles we encounter on our life journey all work to manufacture an oyster that, if we do our inner work, forms a pearl. This pearl represents the lessons, wisdom, insight, and intuition we cultivate. Whenever I have a client who goes through the foundational learnings of NI (the Re-Claiming Journey) and the experiential aspects of NI (the Re-Claiming Process), I tell them that their contribution is to pay it forward. My hope is that they feel inspired to become a MEL influencer who generously shares their pearl to assist their committed love partner, children, family, friends, colleagues, and others so that we can all access our own MEL to serve the greater good.

A Quick Refresher

If you read or listened to volume 1 and completed the exercises, you have already begun to bring that which was unconscious to your conscious awareness. You gained the foundational knowledge of how your meaning-machine mind operates. Accordingly, you have laid the groundwork to give yourself the best chance of success as you make your way through the various steps of volume 2.

In volume 1, you gained valuable knowledge about your inner world by being open and honest with yourself as you completed each of the exercises. Your answers helped you understand and identify your:

- attachment style and the impact this had on your development and may still have on your present life;
- primal attachment needs and how your inner world was impacted when you perceived—real or imagined—that they were threatened, violated, or ruptured;
- adopted or adapted roles, which are the personae you created in your childhood in response to a stressful environment;
- INEs and NUBs that you sense still have an adverse impact on your present-day life;
- red (disempowered) references that have an undue influence on your life today;
- context-related, disempowered beliefs you created long ago that you filter your perceptions through today;
- Core Identity Cycle and the painful emotions and disempowered beliefs embedded within its patterns;
- Triggered Protective Cycle and the multiple components within it;
- top five PODS and their favorite weapons of choice; and
- codependent tendencies.

We'll build on all that awareness in volume 2, where you'll learn new strategies, tools, and techniques—and where you'll answer exploratory questions and engage in exercises in each of the chapters. The questions and exercises provide you with the opportunity to reflect, integrate your learning, apply your awareness from volume 1, and begin to work on resolving the challenges and disempowered patterns you have identified. You'll be encouraged to focus your TEA on the process of healing and growing—which you'll hopefully also find fun and rewarding!

I invite you to write your answers in the spaces provided in this book, in your journal, or on a digital device. How much you choose to do is up to you. You may wish to read or listen to this book all the way through before doing the exercises; you may wish to answer all the questions, some, or none. As a reminder, all the strategies, tools, techniques, questions, and exercises were deliberately designed to help you recognize the formation and impact of your inner world. They are meant to lead you to explore within yourself and open doors you may have been avoiding out of fear. Each of us is like a mansion with many rooms. Strive to be patient and courageous as you begin your journey to open the doors to all the rooms to explore your inner world.

Perhaps you've tried other paths, but they weren't the right approach for you. Maybe you were not ready to open certain doors that you know need to be opened. While you may feel some initial resistance, engaging with the strategies and tools and completing the questions and exercises will allow you to unlock all your unexplored rooms—so you use your TEA to give yourself the gift of healing whatever is unresolved and growing into the next highest version of yourself.

Many of the questions and exercises are challenging and insightful. Be honest, authentic, vulnerable, open, and real (HAVOR) with yourself. Give yourself the golden opportunity to answer the tough questions so you can see what needs to be seen, hear what needs to be heard, and feel what needs to be felt.

During the Re-Claiming Process, I will often ask you to close your eyes, step into the perspective of an earlier version of yourself, and use all your senses to imagine some of those experiences with as much sensory vividness as possible. This is not for the purpose of retraumatizing you, and I will never ask you to do more than you feel ready to do. Just notice if you feel an activation and sensation in your body. If so, then some element of unresolvedness may be stuck in your nervous system. As you gradually move through the exercises in this book, you'll learn to resolve the episodes of your personal History Channel show, authored by disempowered patterns from the past. You will be urged to ask yourself challenging questions to shift your focus and begin to lead a mindfully empowered life.

I share with my clients that one of the most important aspects of our coaching is for me to get them as uncomfortable as I can. There may be times when you are working on a powerful unresolved memory that causes you discomfort in your inner world. This may occur if your NSI (nervous system index) goes above an 8; here, you sense the painful emotions of your unresolved wound are too intense, and you feel like you may get swept away in the moment. If this happens, break your state immediately by using the anchors of awareness, which you will learn about in chapters 2, 3, and 4. Move your body, use your breath, release the energy with intentional exhalations, and continue to change your focus to the present moment until your NSI is below a 3.

If you're *not* uncomfortable, that means you're not challenging the boundaries of a pattern and likely will not grow. If you get uncomfortable while answering the questions, that's a *good* thing. What makes you uncomfortable is a neurological growth factor—a challenge in your life that is really an opportunity for you to use the strategies, tools, and techniques in this book to effect changes in your inner world and transform your patterns from disempowered to empowered—*if you choose.* Pay attention to the discomfort when it pops up. What's it trying to tell you? Is the trigger about something in the present, or is it the past knocking on your door, trying to get you to pay attention to what you have ignored or not yet become aware of?

What Do You Want to Focus On?

Let's start by getting clarity about what you may wish to focus on as you make your way through this book. I want you to consider any recent or current challenges you have or are facing within your relationships: the relationship with yourself, your committed love partner, children, family, friends, or colleagues. Also, be mindful to apply any of the relevant answers to the exercises you completed in volume 1.

Perhaps you have a fear of vulnerability, a belief of not being enough, or a negative body image. You may have already realized that these fears and perceptions are causing you to suffer. Maybe you get triggered and reactive when you perceive your committed love partner as overly emotional and clingy or emotionally unavailable and uncommunicative. (While you can choose your partner, you cannot choose your family.) You may become triggered by a parent who acts like a child or by a child who wreaks havoc on you and your other family members. You may dread going to work or sense a void of purpose, not knowing what to do to feel fulfilled.

Another area of focus may concern a recent event wherein you know you were triggered and became reactive, causing damage to your relationship with yourself and others. This could be a singular event or a persistent pattern you have been struggling with in some area of your life.

I suggest you pick a minimum of two areas of focus as you go through this book. The first and most important focus should be your relationship with self. Remember, all healing and growth begins within! If you are in a committed love relationship, use that as your second area. If you are single, choose another area that challenges you the most—perhaps your relationship with a family member, friend, or colleague. Use these challenges as your focus of awareness throughout your journey. Following is a series of important exploratory questions for you to ponder and process as you launch into your journey of healing and growth. Please do not skip over these, as they will provide greater clarity and awareness, which will be integral as you move through the sections of this book. You'll notice that the questions are open-ended, which encourages you to elaborate rather than offering yes or no answers or one-word responses.

Be sure to check out the handy key terms and definitions list at the end of this book for a glossary of important concepts. This will be especially helpful if you end up forgetting one or all of the many acronyms peppered throughout this book! A downloadable PDF of the full Language of NI, with an accompanying list of acronyms and key terms and definitions for all three volumes, can be found under the resources tab at www.centerforni.com (or scan the QR code on page 310).

Exercise:
Choose Your Challenge

List the challenges you desire to focus on throughout your journey with this book. Begin with the focus on your inner world, then choose a focus from your outer world.

_____

_____

_____

_____

Regarding the realms you choose, think about a recent time when you were triggered by someone or something and became reactive. Were you triggered by something you thought, saw, or heard? Did someone say or not say something, do or not do something, or did you perceive a nonverbal signal they displayed? Is this a recurring pattern?

_____

_____

_____

_____

When this *shift* happened in your nervous system, what was the body sensation you felt between your neck and groin? What were the distinguishing features of this body sensation? Can you describe a visual metaphor for this activated body sensation (for example a volcano of erupting lava in your heart center, a tornado of swirling energy in your stomach, a cold metallic armor around your torso)?

_____

_____

_____

_____

Describe your *thoughts* regarding the challenge you chose to focus on. Were they empowered or disempowered? What were the red-disempowered key words and phrases you said to yourself or to others (for example, *bad, wrong, unworthy, unfair,* or anything denoting such terms or feelings)?

_____

_____

_____

_____

What were your *emotions* regarding your challenge at the time it occurred? Would you characterize them as positive, negative, or neutral? If negative, what was the predominant emotion (anger, sadness, fear, shame, guilt, or hurt)? How long has that feeling been around? When did you first feel it? How old did you feel in that moment?

_____

_____

_____

_____

What were your *behaviors* pertaining to this challenge at the time it occurred? Did you turn toward, against, or away from others? Were your behaviors rigid or chaotic? What was the frequency, intensity, and duration of your reaction? How old did you feel in that moment?

_____

_____

_____

_____

In the script of the *story* regarding your challenge, did you cast yourself as a victim or a participant? Was your story's narrative littered with red-disempowered language? Were you telling a uniquely similar story in which you were a victim? Did that story serve you or cause you to suffer? How old did you feel while you were focused on this story?

_____

_____

_____

_____

As you reflect on this challenge, pay attention to your body signals and listen to your inner voice. Who or what was knocking on your door, and what was it trying to share with you? What was the message coming from somewhere down below—from that natural, intuitive wisdom that resides in the body?

_____

_____

_____

_____

Do you have any other recurring patterns of disempowered thoughts, emotions, behaviors, and stories (TEBS) that bother you, trigger you, weigh you down, or keep you stuck?

_____

_____

_____

_____

You may have a proclivity for becoming either rigid or chaotic in your reactivity. Do you tend toward one more than the other? How often do you get triggered? How high does your NSI (which measures your nervous system activation on a scale of 0 to 10, 0 being the lowest level of activation and 10 the highest) go? Are you able to become mindful and steer yourself back into flexibility, represented by an NSI below a 3? When you get triggered, is it due to something internal or external? (Remember, it's not always an either/or; many triggers that may seem external are also internal because they activate a thought or body state that causes us to go into anger, sadness, fear, shame, guilt, hurt, and the like.)

_____

_____

_____

_____

When you got triggered, which PODS hijacked your inner world (refer back to your answers to the Meet and Greet Your PODS exercise from volume 1)? What was their primary protective purpose? What were they so afraid would happen if they did not do their job?

_____

_____

_____

_____

Have you associated and activated your MEL? What empowered values can you focus on to become more resourceful and resilient? What would have changed in these events if your MEL had shown up and you made empowered choices to respond and not react? What would it have looked like, sounded like, and felt like to have activated your MEL?

_____

_____

_____

_____

Congratulations! By responding to these questions, you've taken your first step in identifying the issues that you are committed to healing through the powerful instruments of NI. As a reminder, if any of the questions or exercises throughout this journey make you feel uncomfortable, please stop and get curious. Simply pausing to become aware of our feelings and sensations, and listening for the messages that arise, can work wonders in expanding our awareness and our zone of tolerance.

If you skipped over these questions or just read them without answering, ask yourself if you're truly ready to hold yourself accountable to heal your inner world, meet your goals, and step into the next highest version of yourself. If you're not ready now, *that's OK*. Just set the book down and come back when you are; it will always be here for you when you resolve to embark on the inner adventure that you'll find in this book. Only you can choose whether to give it everything you have or go halfway. Please do not judge yourself either way. Do the best you can with what you have and where you are on your unique and beautiful journey.

In volume 1 (page 56), we covered the concept of the four steps of programming. In order to work with our inner world, we need to follow a repetitive strategy that gives us the best chance of successfully reprogramming disempowered coding in our unlimited unconscious mind. The third step of the strategy is conscious competence. Here, we are mindful to engage the NI strategies, tools, and techniques with daily intentional repetition until we achieve unconscious competence, which is the fourth step. Unconscious competence occurs when you have formed and reinforced new neural pathways that serve you and flip your references from red to green.

When you want to install an NI strategy, tool, or technique, or you want to reinforce the neural pathways throughout the various steps of the Re-Claiming Process, I offer you the M3 strategy (which covers the three rules of mastery: patience, practice, and perseverance).

M3 lets you decide to use your time, energy, and attention to mindfully manufacture a MEL mini movie with massive amounts of sensory data; as you do so, you'll be using the NI instruments you'll learn about in this book. Depending on the context of the intention for your particular strategy, you'll need to use the tools three times a day for thirty-three consecutive days. This MEL mini movie can last for three seconds, thirty-three seconds, or three minutes, depending on what you are trying to master.

As you know by now, we are programmed by sensory data from the past, whether it's internally or externally derived, real or imagined. We can use the NI strategies, tools, and techniques with conscious intention to strategically and mindfully manufacture massive amounts of sensory data that works to interrupt our disempowered patterns and grow into the next highest version of self.

Remember, we are imperfect humans, and our PODS will hijack us from time to time. You will not be able to follow the M3 strategy perfectly. When you find you've missed a session or a day, please be kind with your mind and pick back up where you left off to continue your mindfully empowered journey. You will certainly learn, stretch, heal, and grow as you gain a deeper understanding of yourself while mindfully managing your meaning-machine mind and experiencing the quiet mind, relaxed body, and peaceful soul that are part of acquiring neurological freedom.

NI Path
of Healing and Growth

*Be aware of your early warning alarm signal
in the moment you feel and sense you are
triggered and reactive, and a shift has happened
due to the unconscious meaning you assigned
in your living laboratory of life experience.*

*Be mindful to see, hear, feel, and sense your
uncomfortable emotions and body sensations
alerting you that you have been hooked and hijacked
and now face a challenge of a chance for choice,
which serves or causes you and others to suffer.*

*Noticing and evaluating yourself and others,
you choose to wake up your conscious mind as you
sit with the uncomfortable emotions and body sensations
being present, nonjudgmental, open, and flexible,
with love and acceptance toward yourself and others.*

*You witness and do not engage your PODS as you
differentiate and not integrate with the
cacophony of commentators arguing for your
disempowered beliefs and perceived limitations to be true
by narrating a story using red AEO rules and the dreaded D's.*

*You make a mindful choice to honor your MEL values by
applying the NI knowledge, strategies, tools, and techniques
to mindfully manage your meaning-machine mind
and own your personal power by being purposeful
to interrupt your red patterns and guide your NSI below 3.*

*You use your time, energy, and attention
with mindful intention and congruent repetition to install new
empowered patterns that serve you as you continue to
learn, stretch, heal, and grow,
becoming comfortable with that
which was once uncomfortable.*

*You lean into your inner resistance to
prove to yourself that you can do something
you once believed you could not do
and discover that you are much more
then you used to believe you are.*

*You mindfully produce new experiences to
create a new empowered belief, which over time,
flips your references from red to green, which
impacts how you process sensory data in the present
and positively changes the way you now make sense of things.*

—Glenn S. Cohen

NI Lab Time

**Practice and Become Proficient
to Give Yourself the Best Chance for Success**

*Repetition of the same thought or physical action
develops into a habit which, repeated frequently
enough, becomes an automatic reflex.*

–Norman Vincent Peale

CHAPTER 1

The Neurological Instruments of NI

If your emotional abilities aren't in hand,
if you don't have self-awareness,
if you are not able to manage your distressing
emotions, if you can't have empathy and
effective relationships, then no matter how smart
you are, you are not going to get very far.

–Daniel Goleman

When we start the work of resolving and replacing patterns, we begin by acknowledging that the answers already lie within us. NI takes us on a multifaceted and powerful journey of self and relationship evolution that challenges us to learn, stretch, heal, and grow—and then to inspire and contribute to something greater than ourselves. This phase of the process encompasses awareness, understanding, and application.

If you saw James Cameron's 2009 film *Avatar*, you'll remember that the Tree of Souls connects the Na'vi people to Eywa, the guiding force that maintains the equilibrium among all living beings of the planet Pandora, where the Na'vi live. Every living being on the planet connects to Eywa through a system of neuro-conductive antennae. *Sound familiar?* (It's strikingly similar to the way humans are unconsciously connected through the flow of vibrational energy via our mirror neurons.)

So, how do you bring about neurological change? First, you become *aware* of any disempowered patterns that are negatively impacting your life and relationships. Second, you come to *understand* how to use strategies and tools repeatedly to recognize and interrupt them. Next and most important, you *apply* the strategies, tools, and techniques by making a conscious commitment to doing the daily work to ensure your greatest chance of success.

Many times, people read something once, seek help a few times, or go to a weekend workshop and hope that personal transformation will magically happen. I know we live in a digital world where we have instant access to information and change happens rapidly. But, for your inner world to heal, changing deeply ingrained, disempowering neurological cycles requires dedication, patience, persistence, and consistent repetition.

It is important to challenge people to step out of their comfort zones and press against the boundaries of their cycles. It is imperative that people fully understand the strategies and tools for change, then follow through with the techniques and processes to facilitate their own healing and growth. Through awareness, understanding, and application, you use your conscious and unconscious mind to reveal, release, and resolve the unresolved cycles and disempowered patterns. This is how change occurs.

I share with clients that the silver linings in their dark clouds are actually gifts—what I refer to as their neurological growth factor. These are the conditions and situations that can give a person the inspiration and motivation to begin a healing and growth phase. Where I come in is in helping people to mindfully reframe their meaning and adopt the belief that they can use the living laboratory of their life, which includes the volatile substances of present challenges and unresolved wounding, to conduct experiments. Likewise, this is your time to perform neurological surgery in the moments you need it the most.

Pain is a great motivator—and when people hit their proverbial rock bottom, the door unlocks for them to become honest, authentic, vulnerable, open, and real with themselves. Hitting rock bottom comes in many forms. It could be a simple awareness that you know you need to challenge yourself in some way to change a disempowered pattern. You might recognize that you keep attracting the same kind of relationships and realize you need to do your inner work. And of course, you might have a dark night of the soul variety of rock bottom, such as the soul-shaking experience that slapped me awake and propelled me forward with my purpose, which I wrote about in volume 1.

Now, it's time to learn, practice, and build your own personal healing bag full of neurological instruments to begin creating lasting transformation. This chapter focuses on the eleven neurological instruments you will use as you progress through the rest of this book. The best feature about these instruments is they are all readily accessible and can be easily used on the spot. They form the basis for the strategies, tools, and techniques you will be learning in this book. We have covered several of these in volume 1, and I am repeating them here to illustrate their critical value as you develop the skills to address your inner injuries by performing neurological surgery on yourself.

Instrument 1: AI:
So, This Is What I Have Been Missing

Active imagination (AI) is the most important tool we have to effect change. When you look at that acronym, I'm sure "artificial intelligence" comes to mind. However, AI can be much more powerful than a computer system because it relies on our mind's natural intelligence to elicit information through our senses and create new meanings for ourselves.

As you recall from volume 1, neuroplasticity allows you to change the structure of your brain, using your mind. You can use AI to consciously communicate with your unconscious mind. Your unconscious mind will believe whatever your conscious mind suggests, no matter whether it's green-empowered or red-disempowered! Remember, your unconscious mind needs clear orders to follow and loves symbols, metaphors, and analogies. It cannot tell the difference between real, remembered, and imagined experiences, and it has no concept of time or space.

You engage in AI by using your conscious mind to willfully suspend disbelief and believe in the make-believe. It might sound bizarre, but you've done it many times before. When you were four or five years of age, before your prefrontal cortex came fully online, you absolutely believed in Santa Claus, the Easter Bunny, and the Tooth Fairy. Then, you grew up and the environment shattered those fantasies. You developed your critical faculty, which is that aspect of you that distinguishes between reality and fantasy.

As adults, most of us tend to give precedence and power to that critical faculty, but we're still capable of suspending it. We don't watch a Marvel movie and debate whether Captain America can pick up and hurl a car the length of several football fields, or balk in disbelief at the physics of Wonder Woman's lasso of truth, or ponder how *Black Panther*'s nation of Wakanda is hidden from the world by a gigantic hologram—we just accept the fantasy. We walk away with the experience of being invested in the story that was played out and impacted by the meaning we gave to it. So, give yourself permission to use AI to play along and play all out—and don't hold back on your journey. When you are mindful about communicating with your unconscious mind, using all your senses (vision, hearing, taste, smell, touch, and the sixth sense that comes from the vibrational signals we receive via our mirror neurons), you can create new experiences that form new neural connections in your brain. In doing so, you can effect the changes you desire.

In essence, an important aspect of your healing and growth journey is your willingness to let go of your conscious, present reality—what you think it is or should be—in order to reveal, release, and resolve any unconscious unresolvedness from the past.

Instrument 2: VAK It Up!: What Kind of Picture Are You Painting?

When you VAK It Up, you use **v**isual, **a**uditory, and **k**inesthetic sensory data to recognize, interrupt, and install new green-empowered patterns. This instrument goes hand in hand with AI, allowing you to actively imagine a scene and to fill it in with vibrant colors, clear sounds, and an awareness of emotions, feelings, and body sensations.

Imagine yourself as an artist visualizing a scene for a new painting. You know you need brushes and paints of different colors to create the scene on your canvas. You have the power of AI to imagine the scene, and then you can VAK It Up to fill in the details by painting the colors, hearing the sounds, and sensing the feelings associated with that scene. Then you access the emotions and body sensations represented by the scene. This is how you bring your vision to life; it is truly a full-body, sensory experience and not just an intellectual exercise devoid of details.

Here are some specific guidelines for how to VAK It Up—whether you are imagining a scene from the past, present, or future.

- **Visual:** In your mind's eye, visualize the scene as if you were looking at it through your own eyes, fully experiencing it. See the scene you create as clear, focused, colorful, and panoramic. You can zoom out and see the big picture (tree line, mountains, birds in the sky, clouds drifting across the horizon) or zoom in for the fine details (the look on your dad's face as he stands on the porch, yelling at you; the cracks on the wooden railing; the uneven tufts of grass on the front lawn). If you choose, you can use an example from your past, but then add how it would look, sound, and feel to show up as your MEL in the present by creating a scene that depicts your desired future as you achieve your goals.

- **Auditory:** Hear whatever needs to be heard that honors the scene you have summoned. Consider the volume, tone, pace, pitch, timbre, and cadence of the key words and phrases and noises you hear in the scene.

- **Kinesthetic:** Without judging, feel any emotions and body sensations that come up for you. Just notice, observe, and be curious. Consider the location, size, shape, intensity, color, temperature, vibration, pressure, movement, and duration of any emotions and body sensations you notice. (Some people will say they feel numb, but the truth is, if you're triggered, you're going to feel a visceral sensation! If you insist that there's numbness, perhaps from emotional dissociation, you can still attempt to locate it and describe what it looks like. Don't think too hard about it—have fun with the process and go with whatever comes up for you.)

- **Sense what you sense:** Trust your intuition and any wise insights that are coming up for you. Listen to the messages and sensations from down below and what they are alerting you to be aware of. Many clients ask me how to tell the difference between the voices emanating from upstairs versus downstairs. Most have listened to the upstairs chatter for so long they believe that's their inner voice. If you're in a similar boat, first ask if you are judging or evaluating your inner world. The best way to determine this is through the language you are using. If you are dancing with the D's (defending, debating, deflecting, dismissing, or denying), you are probably judging based on a disempowered belief. Second, become mindful that you have a chance for choice, which will allow you to slow down and evaluate the situation through the lens of your MEL values. Are your keywords and phrases green-empowered or red-disempowered? Is your story serving you or causing you to suffer an all too familiar pattern?

- **Be in the scene:** Overall, see, hear, feel, and sense whatever journey you are on as real and happening in the now. The unconscious mind will actualize whatever the conscious mind chooses to believe. This isn't the same as reliving a traumatizing experience. When I'm working with a client, they accept the suggestions I give their conscious mind so their unconscious mind can use the instruments to reveal, release, and resolve the past. They do not play out the scene, but they do associate with the inner world of the younger self and go through multiple steps in the Re-Claiming Process to express themselves and change the meaning of the past experience, which then changes their neural connections.

These guidelines also apply to strategic intentional meditative experiences (SIMEs, which I'll be walking you through later in this book). With SIMEs, it's like I've placed a canvas in front of you and begin making global suggestions. For example, I might say you are traveling through space and time and land in front of a house; I don't say where the house is or what kind of house it is. Abstract suggestions such as these to the conscious mind allow the unconscious to use the instruments to go wherever they need to go.

This is not a passive process, and your part in the process is to allow your unconscious mind to paint the picture however it wants, in whatever way it needs.

When you are on a journey, it's important that you accept all suggestions without question. You want to be able to see, hear, feel, smell, taste, and sense them. Let's say I suggest you imagine a scene where you are lying on a beach in the Caribbean, but you imagine a scene where you are sitting on a rock overlooking the Grand Tetons. The content is different, but the context is uniquely similar. The point is, all you have to do is accept the suggestions and allow your unconscious mind to go where it wants to go and do what it needs to do! In this way, you can mindfully use sensory data to reprogram your inner world.

Instrument 3: Nonverbal Signals: Yep, That's What I'm Saying Without Saying It

Nonverbal signals include facial expressions, speech patterns, body language, breathing patterns, and energy emissions. As I mentioned in volume 1, 93 percent of how someone makes sense of communication is accomplished nonverbally. For the most part, these signals are unconscious responses to external or internal sensory input. Rarely, except when we are trying to send an explicit message, are we conscious of our nonverbals.

While you VAK Up a scene with sights, sounds, and feelings, it's crucial to outwardly express your nonverbals so that you have congruence with the inner journey you are enjoying. For example, if you're imagining being on vacation and relaxing on a beach, but your facial expressions are tight and pinched, you are out of congruence. Without that congruence, your unconscious mind might not believe you, and your efforts may be wasted. Expressing nonverbals enhances the firing and wiring of the information and energy you are creating.

As an example, take this suggestion right now: You are in a state of absolute, peaceful bliss. Now, see, hear, and feel your nonverbals and have them match the blissful state of being.

When we are truly in a state of bliss, it reflects fully in all aspects of our nonverbal signals. Notice what your body is doing. Do you have a big smile on your face? Did a sigh escape your mouth, releasing any tension that may have been there and letting you breathe more deeply? Do you feel warmth in your heart? Is there an energy that animates you so that you want to dance? If so, go ahead and do it! Your nonverbal signals are the detailed codes to fine-tune your inner programs.

Instrument 4: MIND:
Which One Do I Listen To?

Our MIND consists of **m**eaning-**i**nfluenced **n**arrative **d**ialogues that tell stories about us—whether true, false, or questionable. These stories are influenced by the meaning we assign in the moment. Our PODS *love* to communicate their protective purpose through this process. ("Did you see the way your boss dismissed your idea by immediately looking at your colleague and changing the subject? What a jerk! He definitely doesn't respect you or your ideas. That's why this job is going to be the death of you!")

When you listen incessantly to your mind and its constant chatter, you may get caught up in this cacophony of commentators. Your PODS have their own patterns, which were designed to protect some neurologically wounded aspect of yourself. You may have paid attention to their voices for so long that you believe *you* are the voices! This is why so many people have a tendency to integrate with, rather than differentiate from, their PODS.

When you are guided by disempowered beliefs, your mind might cling to a narrative that ultimately sabotages your efforts for growth and keeps you repeating the same disempowered plotlines from old episodes on your History Channel. You have the choice to show up as your MEL, noticing without engaging and moderating your commentators. You choose where to focus your time, energy, and attention—and doing so is the most important skill you will learn to achieve inner peace. Becoming mindful is a lot like imagining a dimmer switch on the side of your head and intentionally lowering the intensity of your thoughts to slow down and quiet the chatter upstairs.

To strengthen your conscious mind, you must exercise your prefrontal cortex, and you do this by using intentional, conscious focal attention; that is, you are intentional with your strategy, conscious of the choices you are making, and focused on what you want, through repetition and attention. This is literally how you change your MIND.

Instrument 5: NSI:
How High or Low Do I Go?

The NSI is a measure for the intensity of our inner world at any moment of time; it tells us whether we are in a green, or empowered, zone, or a red, disempowered, one. The NSI measures and is defined by either an emotion, a body sensation, or the language we use.

The NSI is a way to recognize and share the state of your nervous system. We use a scale from 0–10, with 0 representing no activation and 10 being activated to the highest degree. Let's begin with the emotion of anger as an example. If you feel irritated, that would put you at an NSI 2–3. If you feel pissed, that would be an NSI of 4–5. If you are angry, then that would be a 6–7; and if your NSI is a 10, you're freaking out and losing control. At an NSI 10, you might find yourself raging and screaming, crying uncontrollably, unable to get out of bed for days, running away, or shutting down completely. (Remember that at an NSI greater than 6, you can become rigid or chaotic; after all, there are plenty of different ways to display your TEBS!)

Let's explore the NSI of your body sensations when you feel triggered. When this happens, your NUBs or PODS flare up, and you feel a sensation in the body, usually between the throat and groin. Think back to the last time you felt triggered. What was the degree of intensity of your body sensations? What were you feeling? Perhaps you noticed a numbness in your extremities, a buzzing or ringing in your head, a tightness in your chest, a sense of compression in your torso, or a volcanic fury erupting from your belly.

Let's explore the NSI of your language. Let's say you had a challenging day. How would you narrate these experiences? Do you use high, red NSI words like *catastrophic* or *horrible*, or do you use lower-red NSI words like *difficult* or *challenging*? Be mindful of your NSI, so you do not infect yourself or your nervous system!

Instrument 6: Breathe:
Your Saving Grace

You can use your breath to lower your NSI and release uncomfortable emotions or body sensations. In fact, using the breath intentionally is the quickest way to decrease nervous system activation.

Early in life, you may have unconsciously adopted a pattern of breathing when you experienced an INE, which later formed a NUB. When you are stressed, triggered, or in a state of "shift" as an adult, you usually follow the same pattern of shallow breathing, which traps energy in the body.

Using your breath intentionally helps you return to a state of flexibility instead of entering the reactive zones of rigidity or chaos. It is critically important that you use your breath to allow energy to move freely out of your body. The key is to get below an NSI of 3 as quickly as possible.

During a SIME, you'll be instructed to use your breath in two ways. First, you'll use it to draw up and enhance trapped energy in your body. It's a lot like blowing on a campfire to help it flare up. This increases the NSI of the painful emotions and uncomfortable body sensations, so you can then safely and mindfully begin to work with them. Think about it: When you experience an INE, you are in a high state of activation, which can lead to the formation of a NUB. It makes sense that you need to "wake up that energy" to work with it.

Second, you'll use your breath after you've released the trapped energy, meaning you can now focus on its positive, empowered alternative. Because nature abhors a vacuum, it's very important to replace the disempowered emotions and beliefs associated with that trapped energy with new, empowered emotions and beliefs. During a SIME, you'll be instructed to breathe those new, empowered emotions and beliefs deeply into your body to fire and wire as many neurons as possible to create a new experience and new neural pathways—which also ties directly into the next tool.

Instrument 7: FID:
I Have to Stop FIDing All Over Myself

Your FID is the frequency, intensity, and duration of your nervous system activation. When our NSI goes past the threshold of a 6, conditions become ripe for NUB formation and PODS activation. To perform neurological surgery on the NUB, you need to be able to reactivate your nervous system. This gives you the greatest chance of success to heal the disempowered patterns and install new, empowered patterns.

The objective in many of the exercises I'll be walking you through is to raise the FID of energy in your body in order to fire and wire as many new neural connections as possible. You will use your breath to amplify and magnify the intensity of the painful emotions and body sensations associated with the unresolved memory that got triggered. The idea here is that we are looking to activate the NUB so we can reveal, release, and resolve it and then install new empowered energy and information.

Do you use your FID to affect (that is, use high green-empowered keywords and phrases) or infect (that is, use high red-disempowered keywords and phrases) your system?

Instrument 8: BSI:
So, That's What It Looks Like

Your body sensation impression (BSI) is a visual representation of any uncomfortable energy stuck in the body. When you become mindful enough to use the strategies and tools you are about to learn, you can use the BSI as your first indicator that your nervous system is activated; then you can start using the techniques in this book to change the meaning and your choice in that moment. The BSI is essentially your early warning alarm signal (EWAS) that a shift has happened within. When your NSI goes outside the threshold, you can observe and allow your unconscious mind to present a visual image of the energy. This way, you have something to work with when you engage in the Re-Claiming Process.

The components of the BSI include some or all the following: location, size, shape, color, temperature, weight, pressure, texture, sounds, sensations, movement, and vibrations. You VAK It Up and use AI to create a visual representation of the activated NUBs and PODS in your nervous system.

It does not matter what kind of visual you imagine—whether it's another person, an animal, a ball of light, a place, or something else. I have heard hundreds of different variations; the most important thing to remember is to go with whatever pops up from down below.

Instrument 9: Procedural Memory: What's Stuck Within

Procedural memory is the neurological system that's in charge of the encoding, storage, and retrieval of the procedures (rather than episodes or memories) that lie at the foundation of our motor, visuospatial, or cognitive skills. While procedural memory enables us to ride a bike, drive a car, and hit a forehand with a tennis racquet at a level of unconscious competence, we can also store the memory of muscle movements during an INE until they become part of our unconscious procedural memory.

Many animals do not have a prefrontal cortex capable of higher functions, like reasoning and meaning-making. When they encounter what humans might perceive as a traumatic experience, they simply shake off the energy and go about their day like nothing happened. In one of his workshops, Peter Levine shows a video of a cheetah chasing an impala in Africa. The impala recognizes that the cheetah is catching up to it, so it shuts off its nervous system, goes into the freeze state, and falls to the ground. It does this for two reasons. First, it knows the cheetah will not eat anything dead, so it pretends to be dead. If this does not work, it shuts off its nervous system so it will not feel anything if the cheetah eats it for lunch. In the video, the cheetah drags the limp impala into the brush and then goes off to hunt some more. When the cheetah gets fifty yards away, the impala stands up, vigorously shakes off the "freeze" energy, and trots away like nothing ever happened.

Unfortunately, we humans do not use that natural ability to shake off a difficult experience. Imagine what would happen to a child if they truly expressed their anger, sadness, or shame to a person who was the antagonist of an INE? If it was a caregiver, the child might run the risk of being spanked, reprimanded, shamed, or punished for being honest about what they perceived, thought, and felt in the moment. In this way, so many of us internalize our INEs as NUBs, which have a tendency to pop up in future moments in the form of perceptions, emotions, beliefs, and body sensations that have been tucked away into our nervous systems until they've become part of our procedural memory.

Just like the impala shaking off its near-death experience or a dog shaking off water after a bath or a swim, we too can learn to "shake it off." The next time you feel activated, imagine—or literally begin—shaking your body, flapping your arms, bobbing your head from side to side, and kicking your legs. As you do this, see, hear, feel, and sense the negative energy and body sensations disperse into the air and disappear into the distance. Repetition can lead to unconscious competence. If you don't shake it off, it may shake you up!

Instrument 10: Anchors: The Ultimate Resource

In neurolinguistic programming (NLP), anchoring is the process of associating an internal response (for example, happiness) with either an internal or external trigger (for example, whenever you think about a snake or when you actually see one in your yard), all for the purpose of accessing that response with greater speed and ease. It's one of the simplest and most effective instruments you can use—and most of us are using it unconsciously, without intention. The idea is that we can use anchors to feel more internally resourced whenever we need to be—for example, in situations when we want to feel more courageous, confident, peaceful, and centered within ourselves (most likely, because there are internal and external triggers that could cause us to feel exactly the opposite).

An anchor comes in two forms: body and language. Both forms are used as awareness tools to either associate with or activate energy and information in the body.

The first form associates a unique body response with a unique emotional state. If you do something unique when you are experiencing a peak, elevated emotional state, you can associate that emotion with the unique response. A story I heard in one of my training sessions works to explain a negative body anchor: A client shared that every time he saw his buddies, they would affectionately tap him on the shoulder, and he would become depressed. It turned out that the client's father had passed away months earlier. At the funeral, his buddies came over to him and tapped him on his shoulder, which set an anchor in place: associating a seemingly innocuous external trigger (the tapping of the shoulder) to the feeling of sadness. Of course, it's possible to create a new trigger that replaces the old one, and we can use the same rationale to intentionally install a positive body anchor.

The second form of anchoring associates specific language with a particular emotion. Do you ever get triggered by certain words? When this happens, it's like the addicted part in us is receiving a dopamine hit. When we are addicted to our disempowered story and state, we may re-engage the Triggered Protective Cycle. When I notice my clients running this inner program, I interrupt them immediately to bring awareness to the pattern. I use symbols, metaphors, and analogies to help them set new, empowered language anchors. We must be mindful to use positive, green NSI words and phrases instead of negative, red ones. (As we move forward, I hope some of the acronyms and metaphors in this book become positive, green anchors of awareness for you.)

When it comes to body anchors, I ask my clients to place their thumb between the middle two fingers of their non-dominant hand when they're in a positive, empowered state. This helps them physically anchor new empowered language, emotions, and body sensations. You can then VAK It Up and use AI, as well as other tools, to either recall a past positive memory or imagine a future positive picture. With the image clear in your mind's eye, use your breath to amplify and magnify your system to reach a peak, elevated, positive state represented by a positive NSI of 7 and higher for ten to fifteen seconds.

When you engage in this touching thumb to middle fingers exercise, the positive, elevated energetic state will act like a wave. In the beginning, your energy will rise and peak before returning to its original baseline. When your NSI goes past a 3 and continues to rise, engage the physical exercise and hold it until you reach the highest NSI. When you feel like you have reached your highest intensity, say to yourself, "Double it—better yet, triple it." Use your breath to amplify, magnify, and spread the sensation throughout your body from the top of your head to the tips of your toes as this new, positive state fills up your soul.

Once you feel your intensity begin to peak, immediately release your thumb, which is acting as a physical anchor. Remember, you want to make sure you anchor in the emotion at an elevated peak state for at least ten to fifteen seconds. Whenever you need a hit of empowered energy in the future, fire off the anchor by placing your thumb between the middle fingers of your non-dominant hand. Breathe in empowered energy and feel it spread throughout your body while silently repeating the empowered messages you've associated with that anchor. Most of us have anchored in negative, disempowering messages quite unconsciously—now you have the opportunity to choose positive anchors consciously. But as always, the choice is yours!

Instrument 11: Trust and Allow: Your Greatest Chance for Success

If you do not trust and allow the process to work for you, then you may continue to operate on the autopilot, disempowered patterns that work against you. Whatever you resist persists. This is why this final tool is perhaps the most foundational one. Before you can embark on an intentional healing and growth journey, you need to surrender to the fact that some of your patterns are not working for you. When you stop resisting and start accepting the reality of your situation, then you give yourself the gift of choice to change the way you look at things.

I know it is asking a lot of you to blindly trust this process. I imagine you may have tried different approaches and methods to change disempowered patterns. I ask that you let go of any self-limiting beliefs at this time and allow for the possibility that, if you do the work, the work will work for you. After all, we never know how our past impacts our present until we unpack the past in the present— and that is exactly what the Re-Claiming Process is designed to do.

CHAPTER 2

Anchors of Awareness

*Our finest moments occur when we feel
deeply uncomfortable, unhappy, or unfulfilled.
It is only in such moments, propelled by our
discomfort, that we are likely to step out of our
ruts and start searching for different ways
or truer answers.*

—M. Scott Peck

This and the next two chapters (chapter 3, on mindfulness strategies, and chapter 4, on VAKing tools) cover the topic of *anchors
of awareness*. Both chapters are filled with anchors of awareness for you
to use to become mindful in recognizing and interrupting an activated
disempowered pattern. As you read and study the NI techniques in
section 2, you'll learn to install a new empowered pattern through
repetition.

The mindfulness strategies and VAKing tools are a collection of
prepared processes for you to consciously use your AI to start reprogramming the context of your inner world. Although we tend to
be wounded from the outside in, as we internalize externally driven

sensory data, we heal from the inside out—by mindfully manufacturing internally driven sensory data that helps us rewrite our stories of self.

When you get triggered, you will feel a stimulus in your body. In order to begin the process of recognizing and interrupting a shift, you need to apply the anchors of awareness to be cognizant that your body is sending you a signal for your conscious mind to wake up and pay attention. You have a choice to take the high road of responsiveness instead of the low road of reactivity. In fact, you'll be building that high road yourself!

As you build a new road, a new neural pathway, these specialized strategies and tools will help you become more efficient and effective with your efforts. The more you understand how to practice your new strategies and tools, the likelier you'll come to use them without your conscious awareness.

It's a lot like building a house: I'll give you the blueprints along with the strategies and tools to create your own dream sanctuary. If you don't follow the blueprint or use the strategies and tools consistently and congruently, in the right order, then the house won't get built—or it won't be built such that it will last or withstand the inner storms that come your way.

In chapters 3 and 4, I'll introduce you to strategies and tools to help you achieve your goals when it comes to your healing and growth journey. There will be some that you gravitate toward automatically, while others may not interest you as much. They are presented here so that you have many options to help you with your specific context. The more strategies and tools you have, the better you can build.

When you face a challenge that stirs up your inner world, experience a shift-happens moment, or get hijacked by your nervous system, you need to engage specialized strategies and tools that help you receive the message from your body so you can step into your MEL and intentionally guide yourself back into a state of flexibility and responsiveness. Specifically, the strategies and tools in this section will help you recognize and interrupt your Triggered Protective Cycle.

They'll assist you in making a conscious choice to step into your MEL, recognize your PODS' protective purpose, and mindfully manage your meaning-machine mind.

To grease the wheels and get you accustomed to the practices that are a part of performing neurological surgery on your inner world, the following is an anchor of awareness to help you recognize a pattern and understand how your PODS do their best to provide you with protection. Make sure you use AI and VAK It Up!

Imagine in your mind's eye that you're in a brown, dirt-filled foxhole that is ten feet deep and eight feet wide. Ten of your PODS are standing at the top edges of your foxhole and guarding you. Your big, mighty PODS are dressed in Navy SEAL combat gear, with body armor and big weapons at the ready. Their purpose is to protect you at all costs by convincing you that the circumstances are dangerous, that you must keep your head down and not take any risks. Whenever you try to poke your head up, you can hear the PODS barking orders that keep you stuck in the foxhole of your disempowered pattern.

Now, one day, you decide to step into your MEL and apply some of the NI strategies and tools. You listen to your inner voice and make a choice to stand up. As you do so, you are mindful of the discomfort you feel in your body and slowly lean into the resistance, until you are standing tall and feeling comfortable with that which was uncomfortable. As you leave the foxhole, you look around and notice you have actually been fifty yards away from a sunny Caribbean beach. You notice a lounge chair awaiting you next to the warm, calm, crystal-blue waters.

Doesn't that inspire you to want to step into the next highest version of yourself?

I encourage you to use the anchors of awareness in this section of the book, whether you're hit by a little wave or a gigantic tsunami that overwhelms your inner world and activates your nervous system above an NSI 6. These anchors will help you learn how to become mindful and give yourself a chance to apply the techniques to achieve your outcome.

Leaving the Foxhole:
The Earlier, the Better!

As I mentioned before, once you recognize and interrupt a pattern, you will use NI techniques *repeatedly* to install new empowered patterns. This is how you'll start the process of flipping your references from red to green. The sooner you can recognize and interrupt a pattern at the beginning, the more powerful the disruption of the pattern will be. Let's say you recognize and interrupt your pattern fifteen minutes after you are triggered. That means you may have fired and wired fifty bazillion neurons to this neural pathway, which reinforces the ingrained energy and information. If you can slowly begin to lower the time differential and recognize and interrupt the pattern five to ten seconds after the trigger, you won't be firing and wiring all that much additional disempowered energy and information into the pathway. Of course, this will take time, which is why consistency and repetition are key, but this is how you begin to change the way you make sense of things. As the late Wayne Dyer said, "If you change the way you look at things, the things you look at change."

When the Triggered Protective Cycle is activated, we have, in many cases, only seconds to anchor ourselves before we get washed away and end up causing some sort of damage to our inner and outer worlds. As we learned in volume 1, this cycle has two components: story and state.

Let's review the story side of the equation: Your story encompasses the language patterns and judgments embedded in the script you are telling yourself in the moment. There are three aspects to our language patterns: global message; keywords and phrases; and frequency, duration, and intensity of our nonverbal and verbal communication (which also overlaps with your state). Think of the most recent experience you had of being triggered, as we'll use that as an example to help you understand the story you formed in that moment.

Let's begin with your global message. Before you were triggered,

I imagine the title of the episode of your History Channel may have been green and flexible. What about the nanosecond your unconscious mind received and perceived some sensory data that connected to a red reference, assigned a red meaning, and instigated a red emotion? How did you change the global message of your story? Did it flip from "what a wonderful day" to "I'm being attacked by aliens!"? Was the global message before you got triggered how lucky you were to have this person in your life, and then they became your mortal enemy and the antagonist of your story?

What were the keywords and phrases before and after the trigger? I imagine they morphed from green to red. What was the judgment strategy you used after the trigger? Did you perceive that someone maliciously broke a red rule you unconsciously assigned an **a**genda, **e**xpectation, or **o**bligation (AEOs) to? (Remember, a red rule is something we place on people and situations that describes what we believe must or must not happen; such a rule supports and reinforces our disempowered belief and causes us to attempt to control anything outside of self. In contrast, a green rule is a boundary we set and enforce for what we will or will not accept; this is functional and healthy because it is about communicating our wants and needs without trying to control anyone or anything else.) Did you convict them of a felony crime by passing down a venomous verdict whereby you denied you had anything to do with the situation—and you accused, blamed, or assumed something about the other person? Did you then call out the special forces of your PODS to protect and defend your story by justifying, excusing, rationalizing, and cajoling to prove you were right?

Now, let's examine the state of your inner world when you had that shift-happens moment. This encompasses the FID of your verbal and nonverbal signals, including speech patterns, facial expressions, body language, energy emissions, and breathing patterns. It also includes the body sensations you may have felt.

Can you remember the FID of your experience? How long did it last? How did it feel? Was your NSI above a 6? Did you continue to experience the emotions and body state even after the originating event? Did it resemble other times you'd been similarly activated?

In the moment you sensed the shift, you felt a unique body sensation. You sensed a disturbance, a shift in the state of your nervous system, most likely between your neck and groin. These body sensations comprise your early warning alarm signal that a shift is happening. What message did your brain receive in order for you to have that body sensation? Was it related to fight, flight, or freeze? What emotion was related to this body sensation: anger, sadness, fear, shame, guilt, or hurt?

What nonverbal signals were you displaying in that moment? These may have been quite different before and after the trigger. What changed with your speech pattern, facial expression, energy emission, body posture, and breathing rate? How did the other person who was involved in this encounter receive and perceive this new version of you?

Remember, shift-happens moments occur in nanoseconds—and we need to apply mindfulness strategies to become consciously aware of what's happening; after this, we should practice the VAKing tools to interrupt the pattern of disempowered neural programming as soon as possible. When I work with clients who are facing challenges in their lives, I tell them that our sessions are intended to help them explore the unresolved and practice applying the strategies and tools that I teach them. I continue by saying that the greatest impact they have on their inner world is not in our sessions, but in the moment a shift occurs in between sessions.

When the living laboratory of life presents you with a trigger or challenge, this is your golden opportunity to lean into the resistance you feel and choose to get uncomfortable; this way, you can mindfully apply your strategies, tools, and techniques to become comfortable with that which was once uncomfortable—slowly and over time. It's a thousand times more powerful than when you practice in a session. This is where you truly learn how to mindfully manage your inner world. The work I do with clients merely prepares them so, when these moments of opportunity pop up in the real world, they are ready to put their learning into action and reap the benefits. One of my quotes hanging on the wall in my office depicts this concept: "Healing & Growth—Moment to Moment Mindfully Managing Your Meaning-Machine Mind with Your MEL."

Let's use another anchor of awareness to help you understand how you can interrupt a disempowered pattern after you have mindfully recognized you've been stuck in your foxhole. Imagine that you are sitting in the cockpit of your own beautiful, luxurious Gulfstream V. In front of you is a pristine, mile-long runway that has been paved thousands of times. It is bright and smooth, and you have taken off so many times that you do so on autopilot. You get triggered and unconsciously begin to rev the turbo engines and prepare to take off to follow a familiar, disempowered pattern.

Now for the fun part: Imagine a squadron of smaller propellor planes in the air over your now red, mile-long runway. Inside the cockpits are tiny minions, all smiling and laughing as they release hundreds of ten-feet-high green gumdrops on the runway. One by one, the precision-guided, giant green gumdrops land on the runway, interrupting the pathway so your disempowered plane cannot take off. This represents your mindful use of sensory data in an empowered way, which helps you recognize and interrupt a disempowered pattern before it takes off!

It takes conscious effort to remain mindful enough so that you continue to use the anchors of awareness to achieve your goals and outcomes. In the words of the late Zig Ziglar, "Repetition is the mother of learning, the father of action, which makes it the architect of accomplishment."

It is natural to encounter inner resistance as you engage the strategies and tools in this book. The real challenge is learning how to lean into the resistance and slowly become comfortable with that which is uncomfortable. Many times, clients will say it is too hard to overcome their inner resistance. They say things like: "I just can't" or "I've tried everything." I remind them to please stop arguing for their limitations, because they are much more than they think they are! I ask them to accept that they have been running this pattern for years or decades, to the extent that it has become an aspect of their identity. With patience and perseverance, along with confidence and courage, they can slowly reprogram their autopilot from red to green and easily send their plane into new green-empowered vistas.

It's important to remember as you move through the next chapters that our unconscious mind loves symbols, metaphors, and analogies, so the strategies and tools are filled with them. Also, your unconscious mind loves to serve you and needs clear orders to follow. I ask that you have fun with the next chapters and allow yourself to use AI and VAK It Up so you see, hear, feel, and sense the images and intentions behind the exercises, in order to receive the greatest positive impact possible. Have fun with these, play along, and play all out!

Additionally, as you can probably guess, one of the hardest aspects of this wonderful journey is to remember to be mindful moment to moment. We will not be able to apply our strategies and tools if we don't remember to pick them up and use them. This is where I ask that you devise a strategy of structure. I generally ask my clients to look at something they wear on their hands daily (a ring, watch, or a bracelet)—then I instruct them to assign an empowered meaning to the object so it becomes a structure that exemplifies a reminder for their anchor of awareness. I encourage you to do the same.

One of the important premises of NI is the Law of 80/20. This states that we strive for 100 percent in our efforts and results and are grateful when we get to 80 percent; after that, we mindfully manage the 20 percent we're still working on. We are not robots but flawed, imperfect humans, and we all have our own unique, special brand of weirdness. The journey of healing and growth is a lifelong process. Remember that flow is flexible, not perfect! As you begin to apply the strategies and tools, do the best you can. You are just beginning, so please do not be too hard on yourself or use this journey to reinforce disempowered beliefs. It's like riding a bike for the first time. You may fall off a few times, but through repetition, it will become natural. There is a lag time between feeling uncomfortable while practicing conscious competence and becoming comfortable as you develop unconscious competence. Be patient and compassionate with yourself and enjoy the process!

How Are You Processing: Judging or Evaluating?

This is another key distinction I would like to share as you progress on your journey. When you begin applying the strategies and tools in your living laboratory of life, be mindful for how you are processing in the present moment.

There are two possible pathways you can take.

1. **Judging:** This occurs when you make sense of your present-moment experiences by being judgmental, defensive, impulsive, and closed off to any other perspective. You assign red agendas, expectations, and obligations to other people to try and control their TEBS. You usually end up getting triggered, which can cause you to engage in rigid or chaotic patterns—by defending, debating, deflecting, dismissing, or denying. Basically, the message you convey is: *I know what I know and that is all I need to know because I am right and you are wrong!* This will cause you to erode your personal power, and you will end up reenacting and reinforcing red-disempowered patterns that don't serve you.

2. **Evaluating:** This occurs when you make sense of your experiences by being flexible, present, and nonjudgmental. You extend love, acceptance, empathy, and compassion to yourself as well as to anyone involved in your experience. You are open to viewing a situation without judgment and are curious enough to ask questions and seek to understand another's inner world before you share yours. You take time to reflect and consider multiple perspectives before you choose how you make sense of your perception. You are adaptable when you notice your NSI going past 3, and you immediately engage with tools that help you to

self-soothe. You mindfully assign green agendas, expectations, and obligations to others that represent empowered boundaries for what you will and will not accept.

Directions for Working with Anchors of Awareness

In the next two chapters, following each strategy and tool there will be a set of *exploratory questions* for you to read, reflect on, and journal your responses to. You may also use any information you identified in volume 1 as you engage in these reflections—or any other challenges, triggering moments, or reactive events in any realm of your life that come into your awareness to help you explore your inner world.

The exploratory questions will assist you to dive deeper into your inner world so you can work through each of the anchors and determine whether they resonate with you.

Each strategy and tool will also refer to a set of *global reflections* that are the same for all the tools and strategies. You will find the global reflections questions at the end of this chapter on page 64. They will help you examine, from a higher-level perspective, how you would have used the anchor at the moment you experienced a trigger, and what might have been different if you had. The point isn't to lament what you didn't do at the time or to stew in regret; it's to gain valuable insight in how your reactivity can lead to outcomes that cement your disempowered patterns—and to recognize that you can make different choices in the future when a similar trigger comes up in your life.

You may record your answers using the lines provided in the book or in your journal or digital device. Be sure to take note of any new awareness or epiphanies that arise and assist you with your healing and growth.

Some of the questions may seem like they warrant closed, yes or no responses. This is not the case. Please refrain from responding with a one-word answer. If the question awakens any kind of awareness within you (which I assure you, it will), take time to reflect and write about the experience(s) that may pop up from down below. Does the question spark an awareness of something you need to hold yourself accountable for? Does it lead you to an awareness of an area in your life that needs your TEA (**t**ime, **e**nergy, and **a**ttention) so that you can learn, stretch, heal, and grow?

I hope you take the time to consider each of the questions in depth, as they will certainly surface powerful insights about your inner world. As always, be honest and compassionate with yourself. Practice being methodical as you decide on which strategies and tools you will place in your NI toolbox for consistent practice.

As always, the choice is yours: You can do as much or as little as you desire. Just like any other strategy or tool, if you don't practice and use it, you will lose it. However, I've intentionally designed the journey to offer you as many options as possible, so my hope is that the experience will be both fun and empowering. Even during uncomfortable moments, you will have my guidance and encouragement, as well as the presence of your MEL, who will be activated to offer you the care and support that will get you to the next highest version of yourself.

Let the adventure begin!

Global Reflections

- Considering your chosen challenge, what would have changed or been different had you applied this anchor at the moment you experienced the challenge? How might your disempowered patterns of thoughts, emotions, behavior, and the story you were telling yourself and others be different?

- How would the situation or event, as well as its outcome, have been different for you and the person(s) involved had you applied this anchor at that time?

- What would it have looked, sounded, and felt like to you, had you honored and applied this anchor when you were challenged, triggered, or reactive?

- In what situations or realms of life would applying this anchor in the future be helpful for your relationship with yourself and others?

CHAPTER 3

The Twenty-One Mindfulness Strategies of NI

*Mindfulness means paying attention,
in a particular way, on purpose,
in the present moment, and non-judgmentally.*

–Jon Kabat-Zinn

Mindfulness strategies are the aspect of anchors that remind us to step into the space of *being* instead of *doing*. When you consider the term *mindfulness* in this context, I want you to relate it to being conscious of your choices and whether you are actively choosing to be mindful and intentional (a green pathway) instead of being mindless and remaining unconscious that you're being run by a red-disempowered pathway.

Are you mindfully managing your inner world? In other words, are you running a primal autopilot program or are you manually and mindfully operating a different way of working with your inner world?

Think of the mindfulness strategies as concepts that present you a new paradigm for how to approach the choices you have for managing your inner world. These strategies will also set up the VAKing tools you will learn about in chapter 4. You may resonate with some or all. Make notes for how these strategies may apply to your life and answer the exploratory questions and global reflections for each strategy as it relates to the "choose your challenge" exercise at the end of the introduction (p. 25) or any other challenges that come into your awareness.

Mindfulness Strategy 1: Follow the KISS Method: Simplistically Simplistic

For the first of the mindfulness strategies, I offer you a slogan that hangs on the wall in my office. The sign reads: "We Follow the KISS Method: **K**eep **I**t **S**imple, **S**chmegegge!" Some may have heard a variation of this acronym where the last *s* stands for *stupid*. That word is red and degrading, so I switched to a word I felt was light and humorous to make the same point.

This message is a reminder for my clients to keep things simple and not overly complicate, analyze, logicalize, rationalize, strategize, or outthink the process. The unconscious mind is simplistically complex (an intentional oxymoron!) and cannot be understood using left-brain logic.

So, as you go through the various aspects of the Re-Claiming Process, please remember the unconscious mind is like a six-year-old and communicates using second-grade language. Let's keep this journey together as simple as possible!

Exploratory Questions

- In what realm or area of your life are you not following the KISS method? How might that be causing problems for you?
- What do you need to simplify in order to slow down and get quiet upstairs?
- What challenge in your life are you unconsciously making way too complicated and difficult by judging, analyzing, logicalizing, rationalizing, or strategizing?
- What new, simple keywords and phrases can you mindfully adopt to transform a complicated linguistic pattern embedded

within a disempowered story you are telling yourself?

• How long have you been engaging in this pattern? What kind of outcomes are you getting from it?

_____

_____

_____

_____

_____

Global Reflections

Refer to page 64 and answer each of the global reflection questions to give yourself the best chance of success for your efforts.

_____

_____

_____

_____

_____

Mindfulness Strategy 2: Pizza Theorem: It Ain't Just That One Thing

Many times when I work with clients, I share the pizza theorem with them: Our perceptions, experiences, and inner world are like a twelve-slice pizza. There are many slices and lots of toppings. It is never just one thing that defines our perceptions or patterns. This is especially true in my work with couples. One or both of the partners will focus on one slice and try to direct the discussion around that one slice, ignoring everything else that makes up the pizza.

Through the eyes of NI, we do not use any toppings of judgments whereby we assign agendas, expectations, or obligations to try and control something outside ourselves. This is like loading your pizza with a whole container of red pepper flakes—if you do so, you will only burn yourself. We also do not compare our unique slice to anyone else's. Every single person is uniquely special, and we never really know the true reality of someone's inner world, so comparison is neither accurate nor helpful.

We also do not judge any aspect of any slice as being right or wrong, only as either empowered or disempowered. If we perceive something as a "mistake," we can turn it into an opportunity that opens the door for learning and growth.

Another aspect of the pizza theorem is that we do not use labels. Labels are the scarlet letter that gets stitched into someone's identity; they may then reenact and reinforce this imposed identity to demonstrate that it is true.

Exploratory Questions

- In what realm or area of your life do you tend to focus on a specific content or context and perceive that it's everything?
- Do you project judgments onto a person or situation outside of yourself, whereby you assign agendas, expectations, or obligations to try and control that person or situation?
- Do you compare yourself to someone else in a disempowered manner, which then initiates and perpetuates a pattern of suffering?
- Have you labeled yourself or has someone labeled you in a way that limits you? Do you continue reenacting and reinforcing this label to prove that your disempowered identity is actually true?

_____

_____

_____

_____

_____

_____

Global Reflections

Refer to page 64 and answer each of the global reflection questions to give yourself the best chance of success for your efforts.

_____

_____

_____

_____

_____

_____

Mindfulness Strategy 3: Balance the Brain: Are You Free to Flow Either Way?

Humans have two hemispheres of the brain: left and right.

The left brain is usually associated with characteristics such as literal, logical, linear, linguistic, orderly, factual, rational, analytical, list-loving, nonverbal, unemotional, and rigid. Now, our amazing left brain works wonders for students when they are learning something new, as well as in the business domain and when we need to strategize and plan something in our daily life. The challenge emerges when we become triggered and get lost in the rigid, literal linguistics of the left brain.

The right brain is usually associated with characteristics such as creative, intuitive, spontaneous, artistic, verbal, imaginative, holistic, and being more comfortable with the unknown. It may be disorganized, unpredictable, chaotic, and more emotional than the left brain.

Now, our amazing right brain works wonders when we feel free to use our instincts and flow with our creativity. People with a dominant right brain are more comfortable with expressing their emotions and tend to be more vulnerable, open, and real. The challenge comes when we become triggered and get lost in the chaos of emotions when our NSI crosses the threshold.

The question is: Do you get stuck or lost in one side of the brain or the other? This anchor is intended to help you realize when your pattern is dominant on one side or the other, thus giving you a chance to choose to freely flow between hemispheres.

This balancing of the brain is one I see with my clients who are couples. The challenge occurs when each person in the partnership is stuck in opposite sides of the brain. The left-dominant partner triggers the right-dominant partner with their literal, logical perspective, and the right-dominant partner triggers the left with their emotions and verbal need to share. The trick isn't to project judgments on the other person but to come to a middle ground within the self.

Exploratory Questions

- In what realm or area of your life do you tend to get stuck or lost in the left or right side of your brain? Are you more left brain–dominant or more right brain–dominant in general?
- Are you mindful in the midst of a trigger that you can choose to freely flow from one side to the other?
- If you are in a committed love relationship, how does your partner respond to you when you are being left brain–dominant?
- If you are in a committed love relationship, how does your partner respond to you when you are being right brain–dominant?

_____

_____

_____

_____

_____

_____

Global Reflections

Refer to page 64 and answer each of the global reflection questions to give yourself the best chance of success for your efforts.

_____

_____

_____

_____

_____

_____

Mindfulness Strategy 4: Neurological Detox: One Poke at Time

One objective here is to help you learn how to poke holes in and bust the boundaries of your Triggered Protective Cycle. When you have been associating with some unresolvedness and activating this disempowered cycle for years or even decades, it may become your safe place, your comfort zone, because it has become so familiar. The challenge is to address the energy bound up in this cycle. This energy activates the body and releases neurotransmitters like epinephrine and adrenaline. Unfortunately, some people become addicted to this activated state. It makes them feel energized and alive, even if it causes them and others to suffer.

This is when I share with clients that they need to begin a process of neurological detox. You need to understand that when you begin to apply the strategies and tools, poking holes and making new choices, you will feel an inner resistance. This is the time to lean into the resistance with loving kindness and become comfortable with that which was once uncomfortable. When you do this over and over, you will eventually dissolve the boundary and grow new neural pathways. Remember, mindful repetition is the key that unlocks the door to your expansion and growth.

Another way of looking at the process of neurological detox is the following reminder: "Be kind with your mind." What this means is that when we have been running a red-disempowered pattern and now are committed to do the work to reprogram our autopilot pattern, we need to be mindful of our internal dialogue (ID). As we learned in volume 1, humans have approximately 70,000 thoughts a day, and 80 percent are the same as they were the day before. If your pattern has been predominantly red, the 80 percent is probably littered with red keywords and phrases.

Depending on the focus of your attention, a large percentage of the script you tell yourself and share with others is usually in the context of shame or pain from the past, or fear or worry about the future. You unconsciously become hypervigilant to manage and control your inner and outer environment and become addicted to using your favorite weapons of choice when you perceive danger, whether real or imagined. You judge yourself and others; have lots of agendas, expectations, and obligations; and use the dreaded D's to defend, deflect, debate, deny, and dismiss.

When you make the choice to enter a process of neurological detox, you need to use the strategies and tools to be aware when you get caught by a red, disempowering thought, then keep coming back to the present moment without self-judgment. When you are not kind with your mind, you may not notice when your NSI has gone above a

6, and you abuse your inner world with the toxic thoughts, emotions, behaviors, and stories (TEBS) inherent in the disempowered pattern you desire to detox from.

When you become addicted to a pattern, you need to slow down, become quiet upstairs, and go green with loving kindness directed at yourself, over and over again. You know the old red stories will pop up from time to time as you go through this detox phase—this is your time to step into your MEL by applying mindfulness to recognize and interrupt your patterns. Until you retrain your brain, you know there will be a lag time between when you engage your strategies and tools with conscious competence and when you become unconsciously competent in your new empowered pattern orienting you toward healing and growth.

Exploratory Questions

- In what realm or area of your life are you feeling an inner resistance to change?
- What is the body sensation you feel when you are pressing against this resistance?
- What is your internal dialogue related to this sense of resistance?
- Has the energy you feel when this pattern is activated become an addiction to chaos or rigidity?
- What can you do today to begin your neurological detox by leaning into what is uncomfortable and poking holes in the boundary of a disempowered pattern—until this becomes comfortable?

_____

_____

_____

_____

_____

Global Reflections

Refer to page 64 and answer each of the global reflection questions to give yourself the best chance of success for your efforts.

_____

_____

_____

_____

_____

_____

Mindfulness Strategy 5: You Have Your Answers: Downstairs, Not Upstairs!

I have a sign at the entrance of my office with this quote in a frame: "Please Leave Your Brain at the Door." As you go through the educational aspect of learning the science and sensibility of NI, your thinking left brain is welcome to participate. Once you begin to engage in the process of exploring your inner world and participating in the experiential processes, the analytical left brain is not very helpful (remember the first strategy!).

Many times, people have read lots of books, experienced other modalities of treatment, or been to workshops, seminars, and retreats. I ask that they suspend judgment and begin their journey with a beginner's mind to avoid trying to satisfy the left brain's appetite to outthink the process. The left brain will judge and ponder, attempting to make sense of things by analyzing, logicalizing, and rationalizing your inner world.

I ask that you practice becoming mindful so you can focus on the messages coming up from downstairs and not the thoughts coming down from upstairs. The unconscious mind has infinite wisdom and remembers everything. It communicates with symbols, metaphors, and analogies and speaks using simple second-grade language. We have to learn to trust and allow our unconscious mind to communicate with us without the literal, logical influence of the left brain.

Exploratory Questions

- In what realm or area of your life are you not listening for your answers within and not trusting your inner voice?
- How are you distracting yourself from hearing the messages coming up for you?
- What are the red-disempowered keywords and phrases embedded in your upstairs script?
- How can you choose to ignore the chatter upstairs that perpetuates your disempowered story?
- How can you give yourself permission to suspend judgment, place what you know in a box, and metaphorically put that box on a shelf so you can engage your beginner's mind?

_____

_____

_____

_____

_____

Global Reflections

Refer to page 64 and answer each of the global reflection questions to give yourself the best chance of success for your efforts.

_____

_____

_____

_____

_____

_____

Mindfulness Strategy 6: Primal Needs: It's All About Your Nervous System

In the world of NI, we propose that the nervous system is constantly evaluating our present-moment perception to ensure our primal needs of safety, certainty, and trust are being met, whether this perception is real or imagined. If your unconscious mind perceives that your sense of safety, certainty, and trust is threatened, violated, or ruptured, your nervous system may associate with an unresolved NUB from the past and activate a disempowered pattern in the present.

You need to be mindful that your inner world is consistently assessing whether you are safe or in danger in some way, real or imagined. When you perceive danger, your nervous system will activate the fight, flight, or freeze response. This will cause a physiological reaction in your system that alerts you to a shift in your inner world—namely, that your NSI is about to or has crossed 6, and you are entering the reactive zone of rigidity or chaos. This is when you may truly feel much younger than you are and begin to think and act like a child or a reptile, and your PODS will hijack your mind to fulfill their protective purpose. This is a wonderful opportunity to apply the strategies and tools to grow yourself back up in an empowering way and show up as the highest version of yourself.

Exploratory Questions

- In what realm or area of your life have you sensed your perception of safety, certainty, and trust being threatened, violated, or ruptured—whether this perception was real or imagined?

- What was the body sensation you felt that could have alerted you to this shift had you been mindfully noticing?
- Did you get hijacked by the fight, flight, or freeze reaction?
- How old did you feel in that moment?
- Were you thinking and acting like a child or a reptile at the time you had this experience?
- Can you mindfully ask yourself if this perception was true, false, or questionable?
- Can you give yourself an opportunity to consciously change the meaning you unconsciously assigned to this experience from red to green?

_____

_____

_____

_____

_____

Global Reflections

Refer to page 64 and answer each of the global reflection questions to give yourself the best chance of success for your efforts.

_____

_____

_____

_____

_____

_____

Mindfulness Strategy 7: OWN You: Can You Notice What You Need to Notice?

I learned the acronym OWN (**o**bserve, **w**itness, and **n**arrate) from Tara Brach, the founder and guiding teacher of the Insight Meditation Community of Washington, DC. I have adopted this concept as a mindfulness strategy for NI.

When your unconscious mind perceives that your primal needs are threatened, violated, or ruptured (whether real or imagined), you may sense a shift in your physiological state via your body sensations. This is a great opportunity to apply the VAKing tools you are about to learn in the next chapter to make a different choice. Many times, you will follow your unconscious autopilot programming and slide down the low road of reactivity without a pause. But now, you can apply the anchors of awareness and choose to notice what you need to notice.

When you become mindful of your body sensations, which comprise your EWAS, you can OWN that a shift is happening—meaning you can stop, sit, and be still as you take a few intentional breaths. Then, you can exercise mindfulness to observe, without judgment, the body sensation that is present. Next, you get curious and nonjudgmentally witness what is going on in your nervous system as a separate aspect of your inner world. Last, you narrate to yourself your sense of the feeling and come up with a metaphorical image of the body sensation that helps you understand, validate, and empathize with the messages coming from down below—instead of the distracting ramblings from upstairs.

Exploratory Questions

- In what realm or area of your life did you not previously OWN yourself? In other words, when were you not mindful and hijacked by disempowering patterns?
- Can you identify the unconscious autopilot programming that led you down the low road of reactivity?

- Describe your body sensations. What do you think they were trying to awaken in your conscious, mindful mind?
- How could you have become curious and not furious in that moment for what was happening inside?
- How could you have been mindful to witness the disempowered chatter upstairs without engaging it?

_____

_____

_____

_____

_____

_____

Global Reflections

Refer to page 64 and answer each of the global reflection questions to give yourself the best chance of success for your efforts.

_____

_____

_____

_____

_____

_____

Mindfulness Strategy 8: Nonjudgmental Noticing: Can You See Without Judging Me?

When you are triggered, you need to learn how to OWN your inner world and manage your body with your mind so you can make a choice to respond and not react. You need to become a witnesser of your mind and be aware of your thoughts, emotions, and sensations while staying in the present moment. You need to observe and not engage all the random thoughts that constantly swirl in your head. You need to be mindful that you do not allow yourself to become caught by a random red thought.

We are imperfect humans, and we all use some form of judgment to evaluate the present moment. Most of the time, this process is unconscious and happens in nanoseconds. The challenge is to be mindful enough to evaluate whether the judgment is green-empowered and serves us, or red-disempowered and causes us or others to suffer in some way.

Unfortunately, there are some red, rigid judgments that are prejudiced, racist, bigoted, and self-serving. If we are aware of and acknowledge these as part of our identity, we can choose to examine them from a higher level of awareness—from a place of our MEL being open and flexible—and we can choose to reveal, release, and resolve the context from the past where these red judgments were formed and change them in ways that will honor ourselves and others.

How you assign meaning and what beliefs you choose to operate under are your right and choice—no judgment. I ask that, as you practice these mindfulness strategies, you give yourself an opportunity to choose to notice when you may be assigning a disempowered judgment to your experience. From there, you can reevaluate any embedded patterns from the past so you can be more nonjudgmental in the present.

Exploratory Questions

- In what realm or area of your life did you not notice that your judgments were disempowered?
- What agendas, expectations, or obligations did you assign to someone to try and control what they perceived, thought, said, or did?
- What verdict did you pass on them while also denying you had nothing to do with this? In what way did you accuse, blame, or make assumptions about their perceptions, thoughts, and feelings?
- What was your pattern of protecting your story by justifying, excusing, rationalizing, or cajoling to prove, no matter what, that you were absolutely right?
- How has this strategy been working for you?

_____

_____

_____

_____

_____

_____

Global Reflections

Refer to page 64 and answer each of the global reflection questions to give yourself the best chance of success for your efforts.

_____

_____

_____

_____

_____

_____

Mindfulness Strategy 9: Stop, Sit, Be Still: Take a Break and Cop a Squat

When you are in the thrall of judgments, you may become triggered, and your PODS may hijack your inner world. This is when you risk losing flexibility and going into the reactive zones of rigidity or chaos. You may be activated at a high level or in a full-blown state of shift. When this occurs, your body will feel energized or immobilized, and your thoughts might be racing or lost in the muck. This is the time to become mindful of the state of your inner world and apply your newly discovered strategies and tools to slow down and shut up upstairs.

One important awareness anchor is to stop, sit, and be still. When we're in the spiral of a shift, it's a challenge to sense when to stop—and then, if possible, to sit, take a break, and catch your breath. But these are the moments in which you must learn to do exactly that! Remember, the real challenge is employing the strategies and tools to give yourself time to allow your body to self-soothe and get your NSI below 3 _in the times when you feel most uncomfortable._ This is all for the purpose of learning to become more comfortable over time with difficult emotions and body sensations.

When you do feel a sense of unease in the body, this is the time for you to break your state and begin to manage your inner world. This is the time to let go and allow flow—because you know that whatever you resist persists and whatever you focus on, you feel. Focus on your breath in the present moment. When your mind tries to distract you with a thought that pops up, try to observe it without engaging. Then, intentionally return your attention to the present without judgment and with loving kindness.

Exploratory Questions

- In what realm or area of your life were you not being mindful to stop, sit, and be still?
- When you got triggered, did you feel energized or immobilized? And were your thoughts racing or lost in the muck?
- What was the emotion or body sensation that alerted you to take a break, cop a squat, take a few deep breaths, and reevaluate the meaning you assigned that caused the shift to happen?
- What could you do to remain mindful of your body when it sends you a shift signal, so you can slow way down and shut up upstairs?
- Have you ever intentionally self-soothed your nervous system back below a 3 when you were triggered?
- What would it feel like to be able to manage your mind to achieve that goal?

_____

_____

_____

_____

_____

Global Reflections

Refer to page 64 and answer each of the global reflection questions to give yourself the best chance of success for your efforts.

_____

_____

_____

_____

_____

_____

Mindfulness Strategy 10: Intentional Breathing: A Free Tool You Can Always Use

When you choose to take a break and cop a squat, you are honoring your body—your inner world. When you are triggered, hijacked, or have a shift happen, you may instantly begin a process of shallow breathing. In that moment, you're trapping the reactive energy in your body and shoving it back down instead of allowing it to be released.

Intentional breathing allows energy to flow freely within and out of your body; the best part is, you can use it anytime and anywhere! When you are triggered, you will metaphorically tap into a reservoir of stuck energy in your body; you will then use your breath to keep your body open, allow energy to flow, and listen for the messages from below.

One of the most important strategies I share with my clients is the 4-6-8 intentional breathing technique. Once you choose to stop, sit, and be still, you can engage in this critical technique.

You begin by taking a deep inhalation for _four seconds_. Next, you hold your breath for _six seconds_ before slowly exhaling for _eight seconds_. Make an audible sound of relief when you are exhaling, which allows more energy to move through your vocal cords. Repeat this technique five times and witness how it quiets your mind and calms your body.

In the next chapter on VAKing tools, I will present additional tools to use on your intentional exhalations. You'll use AI to create a BSI of the energy in your body. You will VAK It Up to see, hear, feel, and sense any uncomfortable emotions or body sensations leaving your body, dispersing into the air, and most importantly, disappearing into the distance.

The 4-6-8 intentional breathing technique is an empowered command from the conscious mind to the unconscious mind to let go and release uncomfortable emotions or body sensations. The more you engage it over time, the quicker you'll see your patterns dissipating before your eyes.

Exploratory Questions

- In what realm or area of your life are you not mindful of your shallow breathing?
- Are you mindful when you stuff and swallow painful emotions and don't allow yourself to mindfully express yourself?
- Have you ever used a breathing technique to lower your NSI below a 3?
- Can you try right now to follow the directions for the 4-6-8 Intentional breathing technique for five rounds?
- What was that like for you?

_____

_____

_____

_____

_____

_____

Global Reflections

Refer to page 64 and answer each of the global reflection questions to give yourself the best chance of success for your efforts.

_____

_____

_____

_____

_____

Mindfulness Strategy 11: Mirror of Judgment: We Project That Which We Protect

A fascinating aspect of humans is our innate ability to perceive others through the signals received via our mirror neurons. As we experience the present moment, the people we encounter may become mirrors reflecting back to us some aspect of unresolvedness in our own inner world. This could trigger us and cause a sense of discomfort within.

Perception is projection is a topic I covered in volume 1. In essence, our unconscious mind may perceive in others a trait, state, or pattern that awakens some unresolvedness within us. This causes us to feel uncomfortable, and we then metaphorically grab that discomfort and toss it back to the other person. *We project that which we protect.* We are not able to consciously admit or accept these disempowered aspects of self and end up allowing them to hijack our inner world.

When you can mindfully OWN your inner world and stop, sit, and be still by employing intentional breaths, you give yourself a chance for choice. You can then reevaluate the unconscious judgment you projected via your perception. It is in that moment that you can recognize and interrupt a disempowered pattern and begin to look within to better understand the deeper aspect of your unconscious programming and where you need to focus your healing and growth.

Exploratory Questions

- In what realm or area of your life are you able to see how other people act as mirrors that trigger your unresolvedness?
- Are you aware of when you are unconsciously projecting onto others and who is holding up the mirror to you?
- What painful emotion or disempowered belief are you protecting that leads you to project onto others?
- What disempowered aspects of yourself do you need to consciously admit to or accept as being perfectly imperfect as you own your unique special brand of weirdness and be totally OK with it?
- What disempowered pattern of projection will you mindfully focus on as you continue your journey of healing and growth?

_____

_____

_____

_____

_____

Global Reflections

Refer to page 64 and answer each of the global reflection questions to give yourself the best chance of success for your efforts.

_____

_____

_____

_____

_____

Mindfulness Strategy 12: Hooked and Hijacked: Let Go of Your Red AEOs

When you consciously or unconsciously assign a disempowered judgment to something or someone, you are usually projecting something you are protecting. Your PODS' primary protective purpose is to engage a strategy to guard the gates of your inner world. Disempowered judgments are one of their primary weapons of choice.

When you judge yourself and others in this way, you feed your PODS superfood. PODS absolutely love to devour and spit out disempowered judgments. Judgments begin when you assign a red **a**genda, **e**xpectation, or **o**bligation (AEO). These are rules we use to try to control someone or something outside of the self. When your red AEO rule is broken, you will feel pain in some way. You then pass down venomous verdicts and validate the PODS' roles by defending your story.

You can tell when someone has been hooked and hijacked when you pay attention to their nonverbals and the keywords and phrases within the script of the story they are sharing. Usually, with the process of judgments, you can hear the PODS dancing with the dreaded *D*'s. When PODS engage this process and dance with the *D*'s, people usually become reactive instead of responsive, furious instead of curious.

Being hooked and hijacked is a lot like driving a car. You're enjoying a ride through the mountains when suddenly, out of nowhere, a giant red Mack truck starts riding your bumper. As you focus your attention on the truck in your rearview mirror, you are likely to fly off the road, get into a wreck, and cause damage to yourself and others.

If you've ever watched the movie *Little Shop of Horrors*, you may recall that the character Seymour (played by Rick Moranis) was confronted by a giant Venus flytrap demanding, "Feed me, Seymour, feed me!" That is precisely what happens when your PODS come out to play. They want you to feed them by jabbing others with the dreaded *D*'s and assigning red AEOs onto yourself or others.

When you use the mindfulness strategies you have already learned, you can choose to release your red rules of trying to control someone or something in your outer world and be mindful to nourish your inner world with green rules, which represent boundaries you have chosen with respect to what you will and won't accept from others and how you will treat yourself. Remember, the more red rules you have, the harder it is to be happy.

Exploratory Questions

- In what realm or area of your life did your nervous system get hooked and hijacked?
- What were you protecting, and who or what were you perceiving, that led you to become reactive and have your inner world hijacked?
- What red AEO rules did you assign to try and control someone or something outside of yourself?
- Who or what was the locus of your focus for these rules?
- When you were hooked and hijacked, what were the red keywords and phrases within the script of your story that you used to prove you were right, no matter what the consequences were?
- Which of the dreaded *D*'s are your favorite weapons: defending, debating, deflecting, dismissing, or denying?

Global Reflections

Refer to page 64 and answer each of the global reflection questions to give yourself the best chance of success for your efforts.

_____

_____

_____

_____

_____

_____

Mindfulness Strategy 13:
Neurological Growth Questions:
It's What, Not Why

When you get triggered and have a shift happen, your PODS might hijack your inner world. They will follow their protective purpose, employ their weapons of red judgments, and dance with the _D_'s. After a neurologically intense period of time, you could hit your rock bottom. At this point, you might say, "Enough is enough! I cannot keep doing this!"

In the _journey of life_ concept covered in volume 1, the proverbial rock bottom marks a point when you face a small, medium, large, or extra-large challenge where you must choose to make sense of where you are. Do you choose to live at cause or effect, focus on what you want or do not want, get your neurological needs met positively or negatively, employ inner dialogue using language that is green or red? All this will determine whether you remain in a state of suffering or use your experience to serve as a neurological growth factor. The language of the questions you ask yourself will determine whether you remain stuck, regress, or evolve.

Of course, when you find yourself in this predicament, there are two very different inquiry paths you can choose. Many will opt to begin their inquiry process by asking "Why?"—why me, why now, and so forth. This is a waste of your time, energy, and attention. Asking why will keep you stuck in your left brain in a futile attempt to analyze, logicalize, and rationalize the why. Instead, I offer you the empowered inquiry of asking yourself: "What now?" When you ask this question, you can evaluate three variables that help you focus on the solution, not the problem.

1. **Meaning: Flip the Script.** "What was the red-disempowered meaning I assigned? What green-empowered meaning can I choose to reframe the meaning so it serves to inspire me to move forward and focus on what I do want in order to grow into the next highest version of myself?"

2. **Learnings: Lock It In.** "What life learning lessons am I supposed to acquire from this living laboratory experience that is trying to teach me something? What are the pearls of wisdom and knowledge I can gain from this experience?"

3. **Values: Fill 'Er Up.** "What are the mindful empowered values I need to resource to become more resilient? At the time, what empowered values did I not have access to when my PODS intervened? Can I focus on resourcing these values so I will be prepared to mindfully employ the strategies and tools I am learning?"

Exploratory Questions

- In what realm or area of your life did you ask *why* instead of *what*?
- Have you recently or are you currently facing a small, medium, large, or extra-large challenge?
- How did you or how are you currently choosing to make sense of your rock bottom?
- Are you choosing to live at cause or effect, focusing on what you want or do not want, getting your neurological needs met

positively or negatively, employing red or green language in your narrative?

- What new, green-empowered meaning can you choose to assign that leads you to be flexible, evolve, and grow?
- What are the life learning lessons you can acquire for future guidance?
- What empowered values can you mindfully resource to become more resilient when the next challenge comes along?

_____

_____

_____

_____

_____

_____

Global Reflections

Refer to page 64 and answer each of the global reflection questions to give yourself the best chance of success for your efforts.

_____

_____

_____

_____

_____

_____

Mindfulness Strategy 14:
Mindful Linguistic Technique:
Protect Your ID!

When you consider all the mindfulness strategies you have learned so far, there is one common element that connects them together: the language you use, consciously and mostly unconsciously, embedded in the story you are telling yourself in the moment.

When you think of the term *ID*, I imagine your first thought is your online identity. We are all concerned about our personal data remaining private and secure. We take intentional steps to ensure its protection. However, our other ID—our **i**nternal **d**ialogue—is the most precious thing we own. The language we use to describe our perceptions and the story we tell ourselves and others is connected to the meaning we have assigned to situations and experiences.

Language describes our perception of these situations and experiences, and thus, our associated beliefs. When you use red-disempowered keywords and phrases, you infect your inner software's programming. When your PODS activate and step up to protect, you will hear the cacophony of upstairs commentators drowning out your downstairs voice of wisdom and intuition. And of course, your various PODS love to mess with you. They yack up a storm by saying things like, "What are you doing? You have too much to do to just sit there and do nothing. This is the stupidest thing you have ever done. I can't believe you just did that!" If you don't become mindful of this ID, you may continue to "shift" all over yourself.

In the process of empowering and stepping in to your MEL, you need to be mindful enough to interrupt your disempowered story when you use high, red NSI keywords or phrases; you must then replace them with green NSI keywords and phrases and mindfully continue this process so you can flip your red references to green ones.

Exploratory Questions

- In what realm or area of your life have you not been mindful when it comes to protecting your ID?
- What red-disempowered keywords and phrases have you used that infected your inner software's programming?
- What have been the keywords, phrases, and judgments from your PODS to create confusion and reactivity?
- How often do you hear the cacophony of upstairs commentators drowning out your downstairs inner voice of wisdom and intuition?
- Have you ever mindfully replaced your red-disempowered keywords and phrases to flip your red references to green ones?
- What were the green-empowered keywords and phrases you used to replace the red language?

_____

_____

_____

_____

_____

_____

Global Reflections

Refer to page 64 and answer each of the global reflection questions to give yourself the best chance of success for your efforts.

_____

_____

_____

_____

_____

Mindfulness Strategy 15:
Unapproved Language List:
Stop Limiting Yourself and Others

We humans tend to use certain red keywords and phrases in the snippets of the script that makes up the narrative of our life. We love to use words that reflect and validate our disempowered beliefs as absolute: the truth and nothing but the truth. When we do so, we box ourselves into a corner, either within ourselves or with others. This is an unconscious pattern of projection that usually results in some form of abuse toward self or others. Be mindful of how you use the keywords and phrases that may have unconsciously become embedded within the story of what you believe and therefore receive.

When you pass judgments and defend your story, you are essentially attempting to argue for your limitations so as to protect your disempowered identity and allow your PODS to mutiny and take over your inner world. When your nervous system is in a state of hypervigilance, you often become sensitized to catastrophize: You will unconsciously use language that turns what is actual and real, represented by an NSI lower than 3, into hyperbolic language in the form of keywords and phrases associated with a NSI greater than 6.

On the wall in my office is a frame that holds my unapproved language list. It acts as an anchor of awareness: when clients unconsciously use any one of the listed keywords or phrases, I take my laser pointer and move it toward the frame; I then smile and ask my client to mindfully choose new language that reframes their message. The following are some of the keywords and phrases I hope you will mindfully delete from your vocabulary.

- All (all people, all the time, etc.)
- Every (everyone, every time, etc.)
- Never
- Can't
- Always
- Won't

- Should
- Must
- Have to
- Constantly

- Shouldn't
- Mustn't
- Impossible
- Nobody

Exploratory Questions

- In what realm or area of your life have you used language that limits you or others?
- What have been the limiting red keywords and phrases in the snippets of the story you were telling yourself?
- What disempowered beliefs did you rely on as the absolute truth and nothing but the truth, no matter what?
- Is any of your red language some form of abuse toward yourself or others?
- What is the story you tell yourself and others that constitutes you arguing for your limitations in order to protect your disempowered identity?
- What in your language reflects that your nervous system is in a state of hypervigilance, leading you to become sensitized and to catastrophize?
- Which of the unapproved language keywords and phrases from the preceding list are in your unconscious dictionary?

_____

_____

_____

_____

_____

_____

Global Reflections

Refer to page 64 and answer each of the global reflection questions to give yourself the best chance of success for your efforts.

_____

_____

_____

_____

_____

_____

Mindfulness Strategy 16: Neurological Conundrum: Stay, Regress, or Evolve

If you choose not to use some of the mindfulness strategies presented thus far, you may find yourself stuck at the bottom or living a Slinky Life in which you make some progress and then revert back to where you began. This is what I call a neurological conundrum.

The dictionary definition of *conundrum* is "a confusing and difficult problem or question." When you listen to the various voices in your inner world, this may create inner conflict, which can pose a difficult problem and create turbulence and confusion within. Your brain begins to spin as it attempts to answer questions that are often unanswerable.

When you are triggered, your inner world feels uncomfortable and you may begin searching for certainty in an uncertain world. The conundrum is the challenge of applying the strategies and tools to consistently and congruently lean into the inner resistance caused by your disempowered patterns until you become comfortable with that which was once uncomfortable.

You must have the courage to step out of your comfort zone and stretch past resistance. You become mindful and understand the conundrum you created within by learning how to stay in a state of flow as you manage your perceptions of uncertainty from a space of empowerment.

Exploratory Questions

- In what realm or area of your life have you faced a neurological conundrum?
- In what ways were you stuck at the bottom or living a Slinky Life, whereby you made some progress and then reverted back to where you began?
- How are you creating inner conflict that is posing a difficult problem and confusion in your life today because you are listening to the various voices in your inner world?
- How is your brain spinning in its attempt to answer questions that are not answerable?
- In what ways are you applying the strategies and tools in this book to lean into your inner resistance (caused by your disempowered patterns) until you become comfortable with that which was once uncomfortable?

_____

_____

_____

_____

_____

_____

Global Reflections

Refer to page 64 and answer each of the global reflection questions to give yourself the best chance of success for your efforts.

_____

_____

_____

_____

_____

_____

Mindfulness Strategy 17: The Path to Inner Peace: Resistance, Surrender, Acceptance

As you begin to understand the concept of your neurological conundrum, you need to devise a strategy for how you can stretch past your comfort zone to become comfortable with that which was once uncomfortable because of the pattern you are trapped inside of since you were triggered.

The journey of healing and growth follows a unique path. When you are faced with a challenge or a neurological conundrum, you will activate disempowered patterns. These patterns are autopilot programs you may have been running for weeks, months, years, or decades. They may have become embedded in your identity, meaning you will unconsciously show up in a way that validates this aspect of your identity, even if it causes you to suffer.

I often hear clients say things like, "I have to get over this" or "I have to get rid of this pattern." As you have learned, language is the key to our programming. I share that it's important to move through the discomfort mindfully and intentionally—not around, over, or under it. Remember, whatever we resist persists.

When you feel resistance, this is a call for you to do your inner work. First, you must lean into the resistance and become comfortable as you activate your MEL. Then, without judgment, you need to mindfully and intentionally surrender to what is in the present moment instead of focusing on your story of shame or pain from the past or fear or worry about the future. After a period of time, you can flow into the space of acceptance of what is and allow yourself to let go of what needs to be released. This frees you from your disempowered patterns and leads you to own your personal power and achieve inner peace.

Exploratory Questions

- In what realm or area of your life have you created a pattern of resistance?
- What disempowered patterns have been embedded in your identity such that you may have unconsciously shown up in a way that validated this aspect of your identity, even though it caused you to suffer?
- What change have you been resisting, only to find that what you've resisted has persisted?
- What is your current perception of the resistance you have felt uncomfortable with? Are you willing to lean into and become comfortable as you activate your MEL?
- What do you need to mindfully and intentionally surrender to without judgment, instead of focusing on your story of shame or pain from the past or fear or worry about the future?
- What do you need to do to step into the space of acceptance of what is and allow yourself to let go of what needs to be released to gain your freedom and own your personal power?

_____

_____

_____

_____

_____

Global Reflections

Refer to page 64 and answer each of the global reflection questions to give yourself the best chance of success for your efforts.

_____

_____

_____

_____

_____

_____

Mindfulness Strategy 18: Is It Real?: Five Tests to Reestablish Safety, Certainty, and Trust

OK, so you are dedicated to using the mindfulness strategy of resistance, surrender, and acceptance. Let's apply that to releasing some disempowered reactive pattern you engage in with your committed love partner. (This strategy also applies to yourself, your children, family, friends, and business associates.) We're going to take the previous strategy a step further, to reestablish safety, certainty, and trust. After all, with mindfulness, you can begin to own and accept your reactivity and acknowledge the damage your PODS have caused to your partner's sense of safety, certainty, and trust.

You have been passing down venomous verdicts because you perceived them as breaking your red rules. You have been dancing with the dastardly D's by denying, defending, deflecting, debating, or dismissing. Your partner is at their wit's end and has pleaded with you to do your inner work and grow.

Now, put yourself in your partner's shoes, and, without judgment, see, hear, feel, and sense their inner world. You may discover that their unconscious mind needs to have multiple experiences with a new outcome before they can believe that the change is for real. They need the assurance that comes with time and consistent repetition for their unconscious mind to regain a solid sense of safety, certainty, and trust. (Keep in mind that this applies not only to your external relationships but also to your relationship with yourself. Initially, your PODS might not respond well to your MEL, who by their interpretation hasn't exactly been around and, therefore, may not be the most trustworthy person in the room!)

Your partner will unconsciously test you about five times to see if the pattern has actually changed. They may poke, prod, or try to trigger you to see, hear, feel, and sense that this new change is real. You need to understand that you must pass the test. If you succeed the first three or four times but fail the fifth test, you have to begin all over again. It doesn't sound fair, but that's the way it goes. Whatever you rupture, you need to repair! Of course, it's up to you to do whatever you feel is the best you can—but ultimately, you can't control what others choose to accept or not.

Exploratory Questions

- In what realm or area of your life do you not show up mindfully for yourself or others?
- Can you own and accept that your reactivity and PODS caused damage to your partner or someone else's sense of safety, certainty, and trust?
- What red rules did you assign that led you to pass down venomous verdicts toward this person?
- Which dastardly *D*'s were you dancing with: denying, defending, deflecting, debating, or dismissing?
- Have you mindfully put yourself in the other's shoes, and, without judgment, seen, heard, felt, and sensed their inner world?
- Have you surrendered to and accepted with empathy and compassion how someone's unconscious mind needs to have

multiple experiences with a new outcome before they can believe that your change is for real?

- Have you been able to step into your MEL's space to pass five tests in order to repair the rupture?

_____

_____

_____

_____

_____

Global Reflections

Refer to page 64 and answer each of the global reflection questions to give yourself the best chance of success for your efforts.

_____

_____

_____

_____

_____

Mindfulness Strategy 19: BETTY: Love and Honor Your BETTY!

When people are caught in a disempowered pattern, they are judging themselves or others harshly, have too many red rules, are not protecting their inner dialogue, and are using many of the unapproved keywords and phrases. This constitutes abuse to self or others. In essence, it's living at effect rather than cause and giving personal power away.

I will never forget the night BETTY came to me. I was on my back porch more than ten years ago, talking with a client late in the evening, and I blurted out this acronym: BETTY! I told my client to envision Betty White's sweet, loving, compassionate form giving her a hug, and whispering to her, "Now, honey, are you **being** enthusiastically **true to you?**" Up to this point, my client had been acting out with red-disempowered behavior and choices that were not true to her deeper self.

When you do not love and honor your BETTY, you give your personal power away. When you give your power away, you do not see the truth or listen to the wisdom of your inner voice. When you do not listen to your inner voice, you make choices that are not aligned with your MEL values. When you do not honor your values, you are not being true to you, and your mind cannot become quiet, and your soul cannot be at peace.

Exploratory Questions

- In what realm or area of your life have you not been true to yourself?
- In what situation(s) have you not loved and honored your BETTY and ended up giving your personal power away?
- In what situation(s) have you given your power away, failed to see the truth, or listen to the wisdom of your inner voice?
- In what situation(s) did you not listen to your inner voice and made decisions that were not aligned with your MEL values?
- What was the story you were telling yourself that led you to dishonor your values and be inauthentic, such that your mind could not be quiet and your soul was not at peace?
- When was the last time you did not love and honor your BETTY?

_____

_____

_____

_____

_____

Global Reflections

Refer to page 64 and answer each of the global reflection questions to give yourself the best chance of success for your efforts.

_____

_____

_____

_____

_____

Mindfulness Strategy 20: HAVOR: Show Up with Your Highest Standards

In addition to BETTY, I ask clients to consider how they can show up consistently and congruently as their MEL, for themselves and others. HAVOR is an acronym that offers a gold standard for how we can achieve the same objective. This standard has five components, each one referring to a part of the acronym.

1. **Honest:** Are you being *honest* with yourself and with others— or are you lying, deceiving, or manipulating to protect some unresolved aspect of self?

2. **Authentic:** Are you showing up honestly and *authentically* as your MEL or as one of your PODS—perhaps a people pleaser, a hermit crab, or a bully—to get your way?

3. **Vulnerable:** Are you showing up with honesty and authenticity to *vulnerably* share yourself—or are you hiding, running, or numbing to defend your disempowered story?

4. **Open:** Are you showing up honestly, authentically, and vulnerably *open* to sharing your truth or your unique special brand of weirdness without self-judgment—or do you close off for fear of a disempowered belief that you are not enough or will not be loved or accepted?

5. **Real:** Beyond being honest, authentic, vulnerable, and open when you show up, are you being *real?* Are you admitting the truth of whatever is being shared to the best of your ability, or are you using your PODS to defend, deflect, debate, dismiss, or deny?

Exploratory Questions

- In what realm or area of your life have you not fully honored yourself or others?
- Are you being honest with yourself and with others—or are you lying, deceiving, or manipulating to protect some unresolved aspect of self?
- Are you showing up authentically as your MEL or as one of your PODS?
- Are you sharing your vulnerability, or are you hiding, running, or numbing to defend your disempowered story?
- Are you open to sharing your truth and unique, special brand of weirdness without self-judgment, or do you close off for fear of a disempowered belief that you are not enough or will not be loved or accepted?
- When you show up, are you being real? Are you admitting the truth of whatever is being shared, or are you using your PODS to defend, deflect, debate, dismiss, or deny?

_____

_____

_____

_____

_____

_____

Global Reflections

Refer to page 64 and answer each of the global reflection questions to give yourself the best chance of success for your efforts.

_____

_____

_____

_____

_____

_____

Mindfulness Strategy 21: Where's MEL?: What Resources Do I Need Right Now?

This is your last mindfulness strategy. All the previous strategies are ideal to use when you get triggered and lose yourself in the moment. When you become rigid or chaotic, your PODS hijack your inner world, and you begin to think and act like a child or a reptile. You have many strategies you can choose from to help you become mindful enough to recognize and interrupt your disempowered autopilot patterns. The one common denominator during these moments when shift happens is that we've lost connection with the highest aspect of self: our MEL.

So, the question is: Where's MEL?

When you apply some of the mindfulness strategies, come back into the zone of tolerance, and regain flexibility, you can ask the three neurological growth questions from mindfulness strategy 13 and then examine which values you need to focus on to become more resilient. Remember, when you can become mindful, you give yourself a chance for choice.

When you associate with and activate your MEL, you are truly owning your personal power. When you step into the space of your MEL, you use the strategies and tools to reveal, release, and resolve the disempowered imprinting and programming of your past. This is true inner freedom: when you acquire the awareness of your chance for choice based on your MEL values.

Below is the list of MEL values I included in volume 1. (Scan the QR code on page 310 to get a downloadable PDF of this list.) When you get triggered and hijacked and have a shift-happens moment, you need to apply this mindfulness strategy to make sure you associate with and activate your MEL, so you love and honor your BETTY and step into the space of HAVOR.

MEL Value Groupings

Being *present* and *nonjudgmental*
while remaining *centered* and *grounded*

Feeling *open* and *flexible*
with an abundance of *love* and *acceptance*

Showing *curiosity* and *inquisitiveness*
while offering *empathy* and *compassion*

Feeling *connected* and *vulnerable*
with a heart full of *gratitude* and *appreciation*

Having *patience* and *perseverance*
while embodying *confidence* and *courage*

Displaying *determination* and *discipline*
while *honoring* self and others with *integrity*

Focusing on *health* and *well-being*
while honoring your *purpose* and *spirituality*

Bringing *fun* and *laughter* into your life
while striving for *success* and *adventure*

Feeling *energized* and *inspired*
while continuously focusing on *growth* and *contribution*

Exploratory Questions

- In what realm or area of your life have you not honored your MEL values?
- Which MEL value(s) do you need to focus on to become more resilient regarding your chosen challenge?
- When was the last time you were triggered, lost yourself in the moment, and became rigid or chaotic such that your PODS hijacked your inner world, and you began to think and act like a child or a reptile?
- When your inner world gets hijacked, do you ask the three neurological growth questions to identify which values you need to focus on to become more resilient?
- Think of a recent experience in which you got triggered. Write about which MEL values you could not associate with at that time but that you can now access in order to love and honor your BETTY and step into the space of HAVOR.

_____

_____

_____

_____

_____

_____

Global Reflections

Refer to page 64 and answer each of the global reflection questions to give yourself the best chance of success for your efforts.

_____

_____

_____

_____

_____

_____

The preceding twenty-one mindfulness strategies are meant to remind you that you can manage your inner world when you recognize you've been hijacked and know what to do in the midst of such a situation. Often, self-reflection is retrospective, meaning it happens after the fact and after the damage is done. There's nothing wrong with this, but it's just so much more effective to address the issue as it arises in the moment.

With the VAKing tools in the next chapter, you can gradually begin to mix and match everything you've learned thus far. Section 2 will demonstrate how you can incorporate mindfulness strategies with VAKing tools into your life so that you can interrupt disempowering patterns as they arise. As always, if you gravitate toward any strategies or tools in particular, all the more power to you! If you wish to put in the extra time and work to really build your NI toolbox, I suggest intentionally applying one or more strategies and tools three times a day for thirty-three days and then switch it up and practice different ones. You can choose to focus on all the different realms of your life, beginning with yourself and then moving into your relationship with your committed love partner, children, colleagues, and friends. Pay attention to how you feel, as well as the results you see. Notice what works and be diligent about repetition! Over time, I promise you'll begin to notice that your old triggers, which may have been the cause of struggling and suffering in your life and the lives of your loved ones, will cease to hijack your life in the way they used to. When you are on a learning, stretching, healing, and growing journey, the road ahead will start to look very different!

CHAPTER 4

The Twenty-One
VAKing Tools of NI

You cannot see the way out of a challenge
if you are looking at it every day from the same
level of mind, emotions, thoughts,
and feelings of the past.

—Joe Dispenza

n chapter 1, I introduced you to two of the most important neurological instruments you will use: AI and VAK It Up. As you'll recall,
VAK stands for using our **v**isual (what we see), **a**uditory (what we
hear), and **k**inesthetic (what we feel) abilities. Now that you've learned
the twenty-one mindfulness strategies, it's time to learn the twenty-
one VAKing tools. Both can be combined and used hand-in-hand,
but they have slightly different purposes. The mindfulness strategies
are akin to the blueprint of a building; they're global strategies that
enable you to reconstruct the architecture of your neurology. VAKing
tools are the raw, specific tools that you'll use to realize all aspects of
that blueprint.

We are human sensory data supercomputers. We have been programmed with incoming sensory data from the third trimester in the womb, and the data has been coming to us in an unceasing flow ever since. Our programming has been mostly influenced by external sensory data coming into our system as well as internally manufactured sensory data that we filter through the references we formed that determined how we made sense of our past.

Well, then it only makes sense that we can choose to mindfully use our instruments to create intentional sensory data that serves us. Remember, the unconscious mind loves to communicate with symbols, metaphors, and analogies and needs clear orders to follow. It has no concept of linear time or space and cannot tell the difference between real, remembered, and imagined. We can step into our MEL and use the VAKing tools to help us change disempowered patterns, heal the unresolved, and grow into the next highest version of self—in a way that is both fun and very vivid.

VAKing tools are anchors of awareness for you to come back to the present if the past has hooked or hijacked you. Many of the VAKing tools you are about to learn will be for you to use inside the gap between a stimulus and your chosen response, which you'll learn all about in the next chapter. It literally takes seconds to utilize most of these exercises to your advantage; the most important part is remembering that they're in your nifty bag of NI tools! Choose to use them as often as you can, for with repetition comes mastery over your inner world!

VAKing Tool 1: How to VAK It Up: See It, Hear It, Feel It, Sense It, Be It!

All the VAKing tools presented in this chapter are symbols, metaphors, and analogies that are meant to express the intention of the tool. You will use all twenty-one tools to flood your inner world with as much sensory data as possible to interrupt and scramble any embedded disempowered pathways.

Imagine I place a poster board in front of you with a large supply of different colored markers. When I make a suggestion, it is your choice to accept it and mindfully use AI to create a scene and VAK It Up with sensory data to help you to create new neural pathways.

When I lead my clients in a SIME, I repeat the following phrase: "See it, hear it, feel it, sense it, be it!" This reminds them to see what they see, hear what they hear, feel what they feel, sense what they sense, and be totally immersed in the experience. This is the way to make the scene as real as possible, so the conscious mind chooses to believe, and the unconscious mind will actualize—it will help us manifest the outcome of these directives. This ends up becoming the basis for all our patterns.

Exploratory Questions

- What realm or area of your life do you believe VAKing It Up could be of most benefit? Generally, this will be a place where you get caught in either the rigidity of the left brain (being overly literal and dancing with the *D*'s) or stuck in the chaos of the right brain (being overly expressive and emotional).
- How can you be more receptive to the suggestions for the VAKing tools you are about to learn?
- What disempowered pattern do you need to focus on as you apply the upcoming VAKing tools?
- How would it make you feel to finally recognize and interrupt one of your disempowered patterns?
- How would it make someone of significance in your life feel if you applied any of the VAKing tools to recognize and interrupt a pattern that has been causing negativity, obstruction, turmoil, and conflict? See it, hear it, feel it, sense it, be it!

_____

_____

_____

Global Reflections

Refer to page 64 and answer each of the global reflection questions to give yourself the best chance of success for your efforts.

VAKing Tool 2: How's Your Mansion?: Which Rooms Need to Be Cleaned and Cleared?

Imagine your inner world is like a beautiful fifty-room marble mansion. Using your AI, can you see, hear, feel, and sense this magnificent mansion? Imagine your mansion has three levels, with the first floor representing the memories of childhood; the second floor, adolescence; and the third, your adult life. You have many fond memories as you walk down the corridors of time. And yes, there are a few rooms scattered around these hallowed hallways that you have been avoiding for quite some time.

These are the metaphorical rooms that contain your NUBs—the fractured, unresolved memory of an impactful neurological experience (INE) that you were not able to express, process, and integrate back to wholeness. Not long after this experience, it was like you closed the door, put heavy-duty padlocks on it, and then created your protective PODS to act as the door's dedicated guardians. No one in and no one out.

To reclaim your wholeness, you must go into each of these rooms. You need to gain your PODS' trust so they can step back and allow you inside to meet the wounded, younger you. Then, you will follow the steps of the Re-Claiming Process to reveal, release, and resolve the unresolved, cleaning and clearing the painful emotions and disempowered beliefs you locked away years or decades ago.

There is one distinction I would like to share: Often, your committed love partner will have an uncanny knack for finding these doors and challenging your guardians. Your PODS will be hypervigilant toward your partner—and you, unfortunately, may end up making the person you love your adversary instead of your ally. I ask that you allow your partner the benefit of the doubt. (In volume 3, you will learn powerful techniques for how you and your partner can help each other repair the primal attachment bonds of safety, certainty, and trust in the space called *WE*.)

Exploratory Questions

- In what realm or area of your life are there rooms in your mansion yet to be explored? What does this look, sound, or feel like?
- What rooms do you sense you have been avoiding for quite some time that need to be cleaned and cleared?
- Do you have a sense or knowingness of the unresolved painful emotions and disempowered beliefs you locked away years or decades ago?
- Which of your NUBs are locked away in a room because you were not able to express, process, and integrate back to wholeness at the time of your INE?
- Which protective PODS are acting as your guardians of the door, making sure no one gets in to trigger the unresolvedness inside?

- If you have been or currently are in a committed love relationship, have you made your partner your adversary instead of your ally?

_____

_____

_____

_____

_____

_____

Global Reflections

Refer to page 64 and answer each of the global reflection questions to give yourself the best chance of success for your efforts.

_____

_____

_____

_____

_____

_____

VAKing Tool 3: How's Your TEA?: Are You Drinking Green or Red TEA?

As you evaluate your moment-to-moment awareness and honestly reflect on the fact that you are an imperfect human, you can accept that you are still able to intentionally and mindfully manage your TEA (time, energy, and attention).

Let's VAK It Up! Imagine in your mind's eye that you are traveling through time and space, and you enter a reverent or spiritual room. In front of you is someone sitting in a chair who represents your higher power, spirit guide, or someone you honor and have utmost respect for. You sit across from this person and notice that you are in front of an ancient wooden table with two ceramic teacups on it. One is etched with green lines and is filled with green tea, and the other is etched with red lines and is filled with red tea. As you stare at the two cups, the person across from you asks, "So, which cup do you choose, and which cup truly honors who you are now and where you desire to go?" To answer the questions you must determine whether you are consciously choosing to drink green-empowered tea or unconsciously choosing to swallow red-disempowered tea.

Remember, TEA is an acronym describing how you can show up mindfully to evaluate and facilitate changes in your patterns around how you spend your time, energy, and attention. When you consciously choose to drink green-empowered TEA, you use your time wisely, manage your energy mindfully, and pay attention to the language of your focus in ways that bring you what you want. When you consciously or unconsciously choose to drink red-disempowered TEA, you end up not mindfully managing your time, wasting and draining your energy, and focusing your attention on what you do not want.

Let's use the four evaluation questions from volume 1 to determine how you are currently using your TEA. Do you:

- live at cause or effect?
- focus on what you do or do not want?
- meet your neurological needs of connection and significance in a functional or dysfunctional way?
- use empowered or disempowered language in the narrative of your life?

In other words, is your TEA serving you or causing you to suffer? If the answer is yes, not to worry—you can be mindful and intentional in using green TEA to achieve your desired outcome and grow into the next highest version of yourself.

Exploratory Questions

- In what realm or area of your life did you choose to pass by a door that needs to be explored and that is influencing the kind of TEA you are drinking?
- In what context are you mindful of consciously choosing to drink green-empowered TEA, whereby you use your time wisely, manage your energy mindfully, and pay attention to the language of your focus in ways that bring you what you want?
- In what context are you consciously or unconsciously choosing to drink red-disempowered TEA, whereby you mindlessly mismanage your time, waste and drain your energy, and focus your attention on what you do not want?
- Can you choose to use AI and VAK It Up to imagine yourself sitting in front of an ancient wooden table, across from a person posing the question about which of the two ceramic teacups you will choose? One is etched with green lines filled with green tea and the other is etched with red lines filled with red tea. See it, hear it, feel it, sense it, be it!
- In what area of your life do you need to mindfully exercise choice as to how you use your TEA and switch from red to green? See it, hear it, feel it, sense it, be it!

Global Reflections

Refer to page 64 and answer each of the global reflection questions to give yourself the best chance of success for your efforts.

_____

_____

_____

_____

_____

_____

VAKing Tool 4: Left-Brainitis: Are You Stuck Upstairs?

If you are not mindfully using your TEA in green-empowered ways, you may end up living upstairs in your brain and forget to come downstairs to connect with your whole being. One of the most inspiring yet challenging aspects of my coaching is helping my left brain–dominant clients become aware of when they are stuck upstairs.

I use this VAKing tool to help explain the concept of being inflicted with left-brainitis. People with this affliction usually live in their left brain, a rigid inner world that loves lists and is literal, logical, linear, linguistic, vigilant, rational, analytical, and orderly. When they get triggered and stuck there, they are more prone to dancing with the dreaded D's. They judge, justify, excuse, rationalize, cajole, and logicalize their story to prove themselves correct. Left brainers also love to solve or fix something and play chess in their mind. This ensures that their true self is lost in an upstairs game, which is a protective pattern. They are not aware in the moment that most of what they have taken as "true" is perspective and not reality.

Now, don't get me wrong—our magnificent left brain is extremely useful in our personal and professional lives when we are working on achieving certain goals; it's just not so useful in other contexts.

I emphatically share with my couple clients that the right brain–dominant partner does not want to have sex with their partner's left brain; they want the essence of their partner's heart, mind, and soul. This usually gets the attention of the partner with left-brainitis!

When clients become mindful that they are running a left-brain pattern, I ask them to imagine being stuck upstairs, unable to enjoy the specialness that awaits them downstairs. They can then imagine a wide banister they can use to slide downstairs where they can become present, nonjudgmental, centered, grounded, open, and flexible—with love and acceptance. Doesn't that sound so much better?

Exploratory Questions

- In what realm or area of your life have you been afflicted by left-brainitis?
- Can you identify when you are stuck upstairs?
- Do you have a protective pattern of getting triggered and retreating to your left brain, then engaging others by sharing your list and being literal, logical, linear, linguistic, vigilant, rational, analytical, orderly, and rigid?
- When you feel uncomfortable and get stuck upstairs, in what ways do you dance with the dreaded D's, or judge, justify, excuse, rationalize, cajole, and logicalize your story to prove yourself correct, no matter the consequences?
- If you are in a committed love relationship, how is your intimacy being challenged because you are unable to connect with your partner in a heartfelt, soulful, and vulnerable way?
- In what ways can you give yourself permission to slide downstairs, so you become present, nonjudgmental, centered, grounded, open, and flexible—with love and acceptance? See it, hear it, feel it, sense it, be it!

_____

_____

_____

_____

_____

_____

Global Reflections

Refer to page 64 and answer each of the global reflection questions to give yourself the best chance of success for your efforts.

_____

_____

_____

_____

_____

✺ ✺ ✺

VAKing Tool 5: Chance for Choice: Don't Take Your PODS' Bait

When you are on your journey of growth, you will invariably get tested. Somehow, a pattern will pop up when you perceive something that activates a disempowered pattern. This is your chance to make a mindful or mindless choice. When you make a mindful choice, you enhance your empowered pattern and continue to poke holes in your Triggered Protective Cycle.

The VAKing tool I enjoy sharing for this awareness is the story of your troll. As I shared in volume 1, life is like a journey on a river. Your mission is to face the river's challenges as best as you can to stay in flow and remain flexible.

Imagine yourself floating on a gentle blue river on a beautiful wooden raft. You are soaking in the sun and feeling the freshness of the air. Suddenly, you notice a nine-foot-tall, gnarly-looking troll fifty yards ahead, standing on the left bank of the river. In its webbed hand is a giant fishing rod with sixty-six lines full of red hooks. The troll stares at you with a sly smile and chuckles wickedly as it casts the lines out toward you. Do you mindfully notice and not engage the hooks as you continue on your journey, or do you mindlessly grab some of the hooks, get triggered, and get pulled into the currents of chaos or rigidity?

If you have a habit of grabbing the hooks, this is the clue that it's time to check yourself in for a neurological detox. Neurological detox is an uncomfortable period of breaking your addictive patterns by being mindful about not grabbing the hooks, attaching a disempowered meaning, and activating the same old red story you have been telling yourself. When you grab the hooks, you are feeding your PODS superfood and validating their purpose.

Exploratory Questions

- In what realm or area of your life have you believed you had no chance for a choice?
- Do you mindfully notice, choose not to engage the troll's hooks, and continue on your journey when you feel uncomfortable? What does this look, sound, and feel like?
- Do you mindlessly grab some of the hooks, get triggered, and get pulled into the currents of chaos or rigidity? What does this look, sound, or feel like?
- Are you feeding your or your partner's PODS superfood by grabbing either of your hooks? What does this look, sound, and feel like?
- How can you begin your neurological detox so you can break your addictive pattern by mindfully choosing not to grab the hooks, attach a disempowered meaning, and activate the same old red story you have been telling yourself? See it, hear it, feel it, sense it, be it!

_____

_____

_____

_____

_____

_____

Global Reflections

Refer to page 64 and answer each of the global reflection questions to give yourself the best chance of success for your efforts.

_____

_____

_____

_____

_____

_____

VAKing Tool 6: Flaring Venus Flytrap: Damn, What's Happening Downstairs?

When you get triggered, your NUBs (and therefore, your PODS) activate. This activation, known as your **body sensation impression** (BSI) is the EWAS (**e**arly **w**arning **a**larm **s**ignal), which we will explore in depth in the next chapter.

When you get triggered, the bundles of neurons activate, and you sense a flare-up somewhere in your body between your neck and groin. In order to VAK It Up, think of a giant multicolored Venus flytrap opening up and saying to you, "Yo, wake up upstairs. A shift is happening!"

I ask my clients to notice when their PODS have hijacked their inner world and realize they are not honoring the standards of HAVOR we discussed in the mindfulness strategies chapter. They will typically sense a flare-up in the torso, which is when they can use this tool to see, hear, feel, or sense the Venus flytrap trying to wake them up to give them a chance for choice.

Remember, the chance for choice always begins with the body. In the second installment of the *Rocky* movies, Rocky is in the middle of a fight, getting his butt kicked. His trainer, Mickey, leans in through the ropes and makes a very profound statement to Rocky that applies to us all. He yells in his gruff voice, "It's the body, the body, the body, the body!"

Exploratory Questions

- In what realm or area of your life have you not been mindful and aware of what's happening downstairs when you're triggered?
- When you get triggered, do you mindfully recognize a flare-up somewhere in your body between the neck and groin, and hear the message that a shift is happening, and it's time to wake up upstairs? What does this look, sound, or feel like?
- Do you notice when your PODS have hijacked your inner world and you know you are not honoring the standards of HAVOR? What does this look, sound, or feel like?
- What are the consequences for you and others when you ignore your body signal to wake up and access your MEL? What does this look, sound, or feel like?

_____

_____

_____

_____

_____

_____

Global Reflections

Refer to page 64 and answer each of the global reflection questions to give yourself the best chance of success for your efforts.

_____

_____

_____

_____

_____

VAKing Tool 7: Flip the Script: Change Your Language from Red to Green

This inner-world work to mindfully change our disempowered patterns takes time and effort. The hardest aspect is to remember to use the strategies and tools to flip the script of your disempowered stories, but this tool helps you get there.

Imagine you are in your amazing modern kitchen, standing in front of your six-burner gas stove. You are smiling from ear to ear while you cook luscious pancakes on a cast-iron griddle. You're wearing your favorite bright yellow, sunflower-covered apron as your family sits at the breakfast table. Now, notice that one side of the pancakes you are cooking are green and the other side red. Will you be mindful and choose to flip over the red pancakes so they are all green or do you mindlessly serve red pancakes to your loved ones and yourself?

When you notice that you are engaged in a disempowered story, you can use your strategies and tools to change the keywords and phrases you are using from red to green. You can choose to ask questions to seek to understand before being understood. You can choose to respond and not react. You can begin the work of slowly transforming your embedded references from red to green. As the old adage goes, "Fake it till you make it!"

Exploratory Questions

- In what realm or area of your life have you not been mindful in flipping the script of the disempowered story you've been telling yourself? What does this look, sound, or feel like?
- How can you learn to be mindful to flip your ruby-red pancakes over so they are all gorgeous green?
- What would it mean to you to let go of your disempowered story and mindfully, with intention, flip the narrative of your language from red to green?
- If you give yourself this chance for choice, how would it impact the relationships you have with yourself and others?
- What are your common red keywords and phrases that you can flip to green? What would the green keywords and phrases be?
- When you are triggered, how can you mindfully remind yourself to use your strategies and tools so you choose to respond rather than react and then ask questions to seek to understand before being understood? See it, hear it, feel it, sense it, be it!

_____

_____

_____

_____

_____

Global Reflections

Refer to page 64 and answer each of the global reflection questions to give yourself the best chance of success for your efforts.

_____

_____

_____

_____

_____

_____

VAKing Tool 8: Your Debate Stage: A Cacophony of Commentators

When you get hijacked, your Venus flytrap tries to wake up your conscious mind to give you a chance for choice. Of course, your unconscious mind perceives danger in some way, real or imagined. Your PODS are summoned and they may stage a mutiny using their perspectives, emotions, and beliefs. This is usually when you make unconscious choices that can damage your inner world and your relationship with others.

This tool assists you in imagining in your mind's eye a debate stage with two long Lucite tables facing each other from opposite sides of a wide wooden stage. At both tables are five combative commentators arguing for their perspectives. On the left side hangs a banner in front of the table, reading "Left Side Perspectives." On the other side, the banner reads "Right Side Perspectives." As you can imagine, the various voices are debating, defending, deflecting, dismissing, and denying the others' points of view.

Here's the deal: As the cacophony of commentators takes over in an attempt to sway the moderator, where _is_ the moderator? Remember, the moderator is your MEL! Does your MEL integrate with these voices, believing they are authentic, and lose its identity to that of the PODS? Or does the moderator, as the MEL, differentiate from the voices, mindfully managing by listening, understanding, validating, and empathizing with each of them? Remember, the choice is always yours: observe and not engage, differentiate and not integrate—or not!

Exploratory Questions

- In what realm or area of your life have you been lost in your PODS' cacophonous debate? What does this look, sound, or feel like?
- What happened the last time your PODS staged a mutiny and hijacked your inner world?
- What were the unconscious choices you made that caused damage to your inner world and your relationship with yourself and others?
- What situations activate your PODS so that they engage in debating, defending, deflecting, dismissing, and denying someone else's points of view?
- In what scenarios do you allow your MEL to integrate with these voices, believing it is your own so that you lose your identity to that of the PODS?
- What would be different if you were able to honor your MEL, differentiate from the voices, and mindfully manage by listening, understanding, validating, and empathizing with each of your PODS, and being present and nonjudgmental? See it, hear it, feel it, sense it, be it!

_____

_____

_____

_____

_____

_____

Global Reflections

Refer to page 64 and answer each of the global reflection questions to give yourself the best chance of success for your efforts.

_____

_____

_____

_____

_____

VAKing Tool 9: Radio: Be Mindful of Your Chatterbox Mind

This oldie but goodie is similar to the debate stage tool. I created this tool over ten years ago, before I even knew what VAK meant or studied anything related to NI. I watched a movie one day called *Radio*. It's a true story of an intellectually disabled African American teenager (played by Cuba Gooding Jr.) in 1960s South Carolina. One day, he strolls by the local high school football field, pushing his shopping cart. The young kids on the team make fun of him, and the coach (played by Ed Harris), takes notice and becomes curious about the young man. The coach is nonjudgmental, open, and flexible, with love and acceptance. Sound familiar?

As the story goes, the young man's nickname is Radio because he loves listening to music on the radio. By Christmastime, the coach and

Radio have developed a strong bond of friendship. The coach buys Radio a new radio, which, back in those days, was a boxy device with just two dials—one for the channel and the other for the volume.

So, how does this apply as an anchor?

Imagine that, right now, you are triggered and in a state of shift. You are mindful enough to recognize the body sensations. Imagine the boxy radio sitting on a speckled stone table in front of you. The radio is your mind. It is set to a bloodred-disempowered channel and is spewing out vitriolic language; the volume is cranked up as high as it will go. Yuck. Now, you have a chance for choice. Realize and recognize that you can change the channel of your thoughts to an empowered station and lower the volume to quiet your mind; in doing so, you turn the radio to a shamrock-green station. You're relieved as you notice that it's tuned to a station that transmits nonjudgmental, loving, accepting, compassionate words.

Exploratory Questions

- In what realm or area of your life have you not been aware of your red chatterbox?
- When you are mindful that you are in a state of shift, what do your body sensations typically feel like?
- What have the consequences to your relationship with self and others been when your radio was blasting and you fully engaged your disempowered patterns? What does this look, sound, or feel like?
- What was the red language being spewed by the chatterbox radio, especially when the volume was cranked up as high as it could go?
- What were the judgments and red-disempowered keywords and phrases being blasted out from your red radio station?
- How can you give yourself a chance for choice to realize and recognize that you can flip your script and change the channel of your thoughts to an empowered station, lowering the volume to quiet your mind? See it, hear it, feel it, sense it, be it!

_____

_____

_____

_____

_____

_____

Global Reflections

Refer to page 64 and answer each of the global reflection questions to give yourself the best chance of success for your efforts.

_____

_____

_____

_____

_____

VAKing Tool 10: Munchkin Programmers: You Receive What You Believe

In one of the first sessions with new clients, I share with them the anchor known as Protect Your ID (your **i**nternal **d**ialogue), which is the most precious thing you own. I follow this by asking them to please be kind with their mind, meaning they should intentionally use green keywords and phrases to narrate the story they are telling themselves and sharing with others.

Many people have no idea about the power their internal dialogue has on forming their patterns and the reinforcement of their identity. So I ask clients to imagine that, in their inner world, there are eighteen tiny munchkins dressed in colored festive clothing, sitting in front of shiny keyboards. The munchkins are frantically keying in the exact coding for every thought that comes from upstairs—the keywords and phrases—to be sent downstairs.

Remember, the unconscious mind will actualize that which the conscious mind chooses to believe! The unconscious mind takes everything personally and needs clear orders to follow. So, be mindful of your mind and the language you are using to describe your perception of an experience. Please send your magical munchkins wonderful green keywords and phrases and let them be happy and joyful as they help program your new green-empowered patterns.

Exploratory Questions

- In what realm or area of your life have you programmed your unconscious mind with red-disempowered keywords and phrases? What does this look, sound, or feel like?
- In what situation(s) are you receiving that which you do not want because of what you are choosing to believe?
- In what situation(s) are you not being kind with your meaning-machine mind, which then leads you to create negativity, obstruction, turmoil, and conflict with yourself and others?
- In what situation(s) can you now be kind with your mind by using green-empowered keywords and phrases to narrate the story you are telling yourself and sharing with others? See it, hear it, feel it, sense it, be it!

_____

_____

_____

Global Reflections

Refer to page 64 and answer each of the global reflection questions to give yourself the best chance of success for your efforts.

_____

_____

_____

_____

_____

_____

VAKing Tool 11: John Coffey Exercise: Let Energy Flow and Go

In the last chapter, you learned about the 4-6-8 intentional breathing technique. Now, we will add a VAKing tool to mindfully use your exhalations to release and transfer out of your body any uncomfortable emotions and body sensations.

In the movie *The Green Mile*, the character John Coffey has magical, curative powers. To heal the afflicted, he inhales the toxins from their body, then bends his head back and forcefully exhales the toxins from his body, and anyone observing can see them. When you feel triggered and sense discomfort, VAK Up the emotion and body sensation by creating an associated image of them. Go ahead, let your unconscious mind have some fun and go with whatever comes up for you. Then, tilt your head back and exhale audibly while imagining a visual of the energy getting expelled from your mouth, dispersing into the air, and disappearing into the distance. When you feel activated, apply the John Coffey exercise, utilizing five 4-6-8 intentional breaths and noticing the activation of your inner world decrease. Keep this going until your NSI is below a 3.

The most important aspect of this tool is allowing yourself to believe in the imaginary. When you see the image of the uncomfortable emotions or body sensations dispersing into the air, make sure you also see, hear, feel, and sense them disappearing into the distance. This is a powerful command from the conscious mind to the unconscious mind that you have chosen to release this energy and let it go.

Exploratory Questions

- In what realm or area of your life have you not let go of what needed to be released? What does this look, sound, or feel like?
- Have you ever mindfully used your exhalations to release and transfer out of your body any uncomfortable emotions and body sensations? What did this look, sound, and feel like?
- Have you taken the time to practice the 4-6-8 intentional breathing technique to give yourself permission to believe in the imaginary as you saw, heard, felt, and sensed uncomfortable emotions or body sensations being expelled from your mouth, dispersing into the air, and disappearing into the distance? What did this look, sound, and feel like?
- If you haven't yet, what is blocking you from using this important mindfulness strategy? What might you be afraid would happen?
- When your NSI goes above a 6, how and in what situations can you use this tool to get back below a 3? See it, hear it, feel it, sense it, be it!

_____

_____

_____

_____

_____

_____

Global Reflections

Refer to page 64 and answer each of the global reflection questions to give yourself the best chance of success for your efforts.

_____

_____

_____

_____

_____

_____

VAKing Tool 12: Go Surfing: Ride the Wave Back Home to Safety

Another VAKing tool similar to and used in conjunction with the John Coffey exercise is to go surfing. When you feel a disturbance in the force of your inner world, you can use this tool to help you come back home into a flexible state of an NSI below 3.

Let's use AI and take a short journey. Imagine being transported through space and time onto a yellow surfboard riding a giant blue wave in Hawaii. You are 100 yards from shore and see Diamond Head in the distance, hear the roar of the blue waves, feel the warm wind on your face, and sense the energy of the emotions and body sensations in your inner world.

The wave is the metaphor for the energy that is activated in your body. As you are riding the wave, focus on your breath and implement the John Coffey exercise to exhale, using the 4-6-8 intentional breathing technique until you find yourself back on solid ground with your NSI below a 3.

Repeat the John Coffey exercise until you can imagine yourself back on land, feeling centered and grounded. Remember, it's always your choice: Surf the wave to safety or get pulled under by the rip current.

Exploratory Questions

- In what realm or area of your life have you found it difficult to become centered and grounded? What does this look, sound, or feel like?
- How would it make you feel to be able to notice a disturbance in the force in your inner world and use this tool to help you come back home into a flexible state of a NSI below 3?
- Have you practiced the John Coffey exercise, using the 4-6-8 intentional breathing technique until you find yourself back on solid ground with your NSI below a 3? If not, what is blocking you from giving yourself the best chance of success to manage your inner world?
- When you've been triggered and had a shift happen, have you given yourself a chance to surf the wave to safety? Or are you running your disempowered autopilot program and finding that you are still getting pulled under by the rip current? What can you do to change this? See it, hear it, feel it, sense it, be it!

_____

_____

_____

_____

_____

_____

Global Reflections

Refer to page 64 and answer each of the global reflection questions to give yourself the best chance of success for your efforts.

_____

_____

_____

_____

_____

_____

VAKing Tool 13: Twister: Observe or Engage?

According to the Cleveland Clinic Lou Ruvo Center for Brain Health, "your brain is a three-pound universe that processes 70,000 thoughts each day using 100 billion neurons that connect at more than 500 trillion points through synapses that travel 300 miles/hour. The signals that travel through these interconnected neurons form the basis of memories, thoughts, and feelings."

Can you imagine 70,000 thoughts a day? Other research suggests that 80 percent of these thoughts are the same as they were the day before. Talk about junk in the trunk!

Let's see how we can prevent getting caught inside turbulent thoughts. Imagine seeing a massive F5 twister spinning above your head with tons of debris swirling around. You can hear the roar of the twister as it makes a deafening noise, and you can feel the wind whipping furiously around you. The twister represents your endless stream of thoughts and the associated disempowered beliefs, keywords, and phrases that get deployed by these thoughts.

Now, here's your chance for choice: You can choose to stick your hand up into the twister and get sucked up and swept away so that you don't make landfall. Or, you can be mindful to notice and not engage and bring your hand back down with intentional attention to what is in the present moment while you notice the twister getting smaller and smaller as it peacefully drifts away out of your conscious awareness.

Exploratory Questions

- In what realm or area of your life have you not observed the noise upstairs and, as a result, gotten caught in the turbulent twister of red-disempowered thoughts? What does this look, sound, or feel like?
- What percentage of your daily 70,000 thoughts are red? What is the nature of the language that is 80 percent the same as the day before?
- Can you identify the predominant red-disempowered keywords and phrases that make up these amazing amounts of repetitive thoughts?
- Have you practiced previous strategies and tools to flip the script of any of these red, repetitive keywords and phrases? If not, what are you afraid will happen?
- How often do you choose to stick your hand up into the twister above your head and get sucked up and swept away?
- How would it make you feel to be able to mindfully notice the twister, not engage it, and bring your hand back down without judgment and with intentional attention to what is in the present moment? See it, hear it, feel it, sense it, be it!

_____

_____

_____

_____

_____

_____

Global Reflections

Refer to page 64 and answer each of the global reflection questions to give yourself the best chance of success for your efforts.

_____

_____

_____

_____

_____

VAKing Tool 14: Mental Monkey Bars: Getting Lost in Your Thoughts

When you get sucked up into a twister of red thoughts and listen to the cacophony of commentators in your head, you are totally distracted from mindfully managing your inner world. This VAKing tool is a fun way for you to think about the continuous random thoughts that constantly play with your meaning-machine mind.

Imagine a giant set of monkey bars, like the ones you used to play on when you were a kid. See, hear, feel, and sense a hundred cute little monkeys swinging and flinging around the silver bars while yakking up a storm as they attempt to entertain and distract you. These adorable little monkeys represent your PODS' never-ending attempt to hook and hijack your inner world. Unfortunately, over time, they aren't so cute. They can mesmerize our attention by causing us to analyze, logicalize, rationalize, strategize, and judge a massive amount of sensory data, which keeps us ever further from our MEL. We might even think we're enjoying ourselves, although we are most likely distracting ourselves away from green-empowered activities and thoughts and engaging patterns that cause us and others to suffer in some way.

Now, there's a bench thirty yards away from the monkey bars, and it's always our choice to integrate with the monkeys by mindlessly joining them or mindfully choosing to sit on the bench as we differentiate and observe rather than integrate and engage.

Exploratory Questions

- In what realm or area of your life do you tend to become distracted by your mental monkey noise? What does this look, sound, or feel like?
- Are you aware when you are unconsciously entertaining and distracting yourself? What does this look, sound, and feel like?
- What situation(s) trigger(s) you to become mesmerized by analyzing, logicalizing, rationalizing, strategizing, and judging?
- Which of your PODS are represented by these adorable little monkeys attempting to hook and hijack your inner world?
- How does this make you and other loved ones feel when you engage this red-disempowered pattern?
- How can you VAK It Up to mindfully choose to notice but not engage your mental monkeys? See it, hear it, feel it, sense it, be it!

_____

_____

_____

_____

_____

_____

Global Reflections

Refer to page 64 and answer each of the global reflection questions to give yourself the best chance of success for your efforts.

_____

_____

_____

_____

_____

VAKing Tool 15: Lighthouse:
Your Focus Will Eventually Find You

Here is another VAKing tool to use when you sense you have lost your way: Imagine a tall, majestic old lighthouse on the rocky shores of Maine. You are the keeper of your lighthouse, the master of your inner world—except, of course, when you get hijacked and have a shift happen.

Now, it is up to you to choose which direction—your focus—you shine your light on moment to moment. You are also the one who gets to determine the composition of the particles—your keywords and phrases—that make up the light. Let's say you have a pattern of pointing your light to the south, which symbolizes being focused on some shame or pain from the past. Or maybe you have a pattern of pointing your light to the north, which symbolizes focusing on some sort of fear or worry about the future. Both these directions are red and disempowered. You will eventually attract to yourself the very things you're fixating on because your focus and language ensure you will receive what you believe. I imagine you will keep having shipwrecks on the rocks of rigidity or chaos in your life.

As we know, we are all imperfect people, and shift happens! So, let's make sure that when we become aware of and live at cause, we have a plan we can implement. Imagine facing south or north into the roaring winds of a storm; you see and hear the lightning flashing and feel the pelting rain sting your skin. Know that you have a choice: You can stay in the storm or mindfully, with intention and attention, turn the ballast of the light back to the sunny, clear, blue skies in the east or west—which symbolize turning toward the present moment, using green-empowered language as you relish and enjoy reclaiming your personal power by mindfully redirecting your focus.

So, what's the locus of your focus as you continue your journey?

Exploratory Questions

- In what realm or area of your life have you tended to focus on what you did not want, consciously or unconsciously? What did your red-disempowered language look, sound, or feel like?
- In that situation, how were you attracting what you do not want—all because that is what you were focused on and your language had you receiving what you were believing?
- How can you mindfully, with intention and attention, manage your focus and use green-empowered language?
- What would it mean to you and others if you reclaimed your personal power by mindfully redirecting your language and focus? See it, hear it, feel it, sense it, be it!

_____

_____

_____

_____

_____

_____

Global Reflections

Refer to page 64 and answer each of the global reflection questions to give yourself the best chance of success for your efforts.

_____

_____

_____

_____

_____

_____

VAKing Tool 16: Red Rabbit Hole: Damn, I Be Stuck Again

When we get triggered and our lighthouse shines to the north or south, we may fall into the proverbial red rabbit hole: When you are focused upstairs, you won't see the rabbit hole and will probably fall in without being aware that you have fallen. If you are paying attention downstairs, you will notice the rabbit hole, slow down, and make a choice to reevaluate the meaning at that moment.

This tool is a reminder that when we fall into and get lost in the hole, we have a very limited view of the actuality of reality. If the hole is deep, all we can see is the small cylinder above and below the hole's red walls—which are dark, scary, and dingy. This is when our protective PODS rise up to guard us. This is also an amazing opportunity to apply the strategies and tools to effect a massive pattern change.

It's possible to slow down and get quiet as you stop the flow of judgments. Imagine yourself deep in the red rabbit hole. Then, look to the side and notice there is a ladder you can use to climb up and out of the hole. The ladder represents the challenging inner work to mindfully apply the strategies and tools to make your way from red to green. Once you are out of the hole, you can see in all directions and reevaluate the cause of your fall. This will help you to begin to learn that you have the choice to change the way you look at things.

Exploratory Questions

- In what realm or area of your life have you fallen into your red rabbit hole? What does this look, sound, or feel like?
- In the times you've been stuck in your red rabbit hole, what were you focused on and what were the keywords and phrases that comprised the language of the story you were telling yourself and others?
- Which of your PODS were present, protecting you from feeling the painful emotions and disempowered beliefs that led you into the hole?
- How would it make you feel to be able to slow down, get quiet upstairs, and stop the abusive self-judgments?
- How can you step into your MEL and do the inner work to climb up the ladder and out of the red rabbit hole?
- When you climb out of the hole and reevaluate the cause of your fall, how does the way you look at things change?
- Which strategies and tools represent the ladder you will use next time to effect a massive pattern change? See it, hear it, feel it, sense it, be it!

_____

_____

_____

_____

_____

_____

Global Reflections

Refer to page 64 and answer each of the global reflection questions to give yourself the best chance of success for your efforts.

_____

_____

_____

_____

_____

VAKing Tool 17: Two-Step Strut: It's OK to Go the Other Way

We all find ourselves unconsciously getting triggered into a state of disempowered thoughts and emotions. We may fall into the red rabbit hole, which is part of the wonderful human experience. We all have PODS that hijack us from time to time. So, here's another tool to add to our toolbox.

Imagine floating on the river of life, gently gliding in the cool waters of a mountain stream. The fall colors are radiant, the birds are chirping, and you can smell the freshness of the crisp air. Unbeknownst to you, there is an island up ahead that separates the river into two streams. All of a sudden, the current strengthens and the rapids begin to grow as you find yourself drifting into the left side of the flow. Here, you sense your body sending a signal that something ain't right.

This is your moment to recognize your chance for choice. When you realize you are going down the disempowered path, you can step into your MEL and, with confidence and courage, paddle backward with a two-step strut to the apex of the island. In case you don't know what that is or can't imagine it, just sense that you're taking a few steps before you realize you've gone the wrong way. You then reevaluate your route and take two steps back, thus making the decision to go in a different direction. There's a great Turkish proverb that speaks to this: "No matter how far you've gone on the wrong road, you can always turn back."

Here, you can make the choice to ask the neurological growth questions to change the meaning you assigned, acquire your life learning lessons, and resource the empowered values you need to be resilient. Then, navigate your inner world to steer toward the calm and flexible flow of the empowered right side of the river.

Exploratory Questions

- In what realm or area of your life have you unconsciously followed a pattern that led you down the red left side of the river of life? What does this look, sound, or feel like?
- When you are triggered, the rapids begin to grow, and you find yourself drifting into the left side of the flow, what do you typically do?
- Which strategies and tools are you using to become mindful and step into your MEL so that you can steer toward the green right side of the river of life?
- Contemplating the situation you identified, when you became aware that you had a choice to change, what was the new empowered meaning you assigned? What were the life learning lessons you acquired? Which empowered values did you resource to become more resilient?

- What was your experience when you were able to navigate your inner world to steer toward the calm and flexible flow of the green right side of the river? See it, hear it, feel it, sense it, be it!

_____

_____

_____

_____

_____

_____

Global Reflections

Refer to page 64 and answer each of the global reflection questions to give yourself the best chance of success for your efforts.

_____

_____

_____

_____

_____

_____

VAKing Tool 18: Bathtub:
When You Drain It, Don't Refill It!

When people are deep in their red rabbit hole or have ventured way down the red side of the river, it's akin to flooding themselves with toxic thoughts and emotions that can be difficult to overcome. It's as if they were in a giant bathtub filled with red toxic water, and only their mouth and nose are above the surface. As they begin to learn about their chance for choice based on NI, they start to create new neural pathways, especially when they embark on the Re-Claiming Process. This is akin to pulling the plug and allowing the water to slowly drain from the tub.

Here's the real challenge: If the tub is somewhat or fully drained and they make a conscious or unconscious choice to reach up and turn the faucet back on, they will begin to reinforce the pattern by filling their inner world back up with the red water they worked so hard to rid from their inner world. This negates the new empowered patterns they worked so hard to transform and condition in.

In using this tool, imagine yourself fully draining the tub of red toxic water. From there, you can use any of the other VAKing tools as anchors to remind you not to fill the tub back up again! (Your next steps for filling up with green-empowered thoughts will be found in section 2.)

Exploratory Questions

- In what realm or area of your life are you making a choice to drown? How can you save yourself from yourself?
- Have you ever felt your inner world was flooded with red, toxic thoughts and emotions? What did that look, sound, or feel like?
- How can you do the inner work to pull the plug and allow the red toxic water to slowly drain out of your inner world?
- If you have done the inner work, how can you remain mindful to not reach up and turn the faucet back on, which will reinforce your disempowered pattern and fill your inner world back up with the red toxic water? See it, hear it, feel it, sense it, be it!

_____

_____

_____

_____

_____

_____

Global Reflections

Refer to page 64 and answer each of the global reflection questions to give yourself the best chance of success for your efforts.

_____

_____

_____

_____

_____

_____

VAKing Tool 19: Bulldog with a Bone: The Art of Not Letting Go

When people are activated in the bathtub, they may be telling a story and sensing a state whereby they are arguing for their limitations. They dance with the *D*'s and rely on red judgments to validate their disempowered story as true, even though it is causing them and others to suffer.

Hanging on the wall in my office is a framed picture of an angry-looking bulldog with a big nasty bone in its mouth. Imagine you are the bulldog gnawing on the bone, perhaps not even realizing you are doing so. If anyone tries to challenge your story or offer a new perspective, you look them in the eye, chomp down on your bone even more firmly, and growl back at them.

I share with my clients who are running this bulldog pattern that they can chomp on that bone as long as they want. However, they must determine whether that bone is serving them or causing them to suffer in some way. They can recognize that the bone is red, filled with maggots and flies—and all it serves is to keep them in a disempowered pattern, defending and guarding their story and causing negativity, obstruction, turmoil, and conflict with themselves and others. They have a pivotal chance for choice here: With loving kindness, they can gently release their grip and allow the bone to drop—aware that they are safe to be vulnerable—and finally let go of this pattern.

Exploratory Questions

- In what realm or area of your life have you not given yourself a choice to let go of something that needed to be released?
- When was the last time you were focused on a disempowered story, arguing for your limitations while dancing with the *D*'s and using red judgments to validate your disempowered story, even though it was causing you and others to suffer? What did that look, sound, or feel like?
- When was the last time you acted like the bulldog with a big nasty bone, snarling and growling at yourself or others?
- What happened when someone tried to challenge your story or offer a new perspective, and you looked them in the eye, chomped down on your bone even more firmly, and growled at them? How did this make you and them feel?
- Visualize that the bone is red and filled with maggots and flies, and all it serves is to keep you in a disempowered pattern that has you defending and guarding your story and causing negativity, obstruction, turmoil, and conflict with yourself and others. What is the choice you will make from here?
- What happens when you release your grip and allow the bone to drop, knowing you are safe to be vulnerable and can let go of your protective pattern? See it, hear it, feel it, sense it, be it!

_____

_____

_____

_____

_____

_____

Global Reflections

Refer to page 64 and answer each of the global reflection questions to give yourself the best chance of success for your efforts.

_____

_____

_____

_____

_____

_____

VAKing Tool 20: Who's in Control?: Autopilot or Manual?

When we find ourselves gnawing on a disempowered bone, we are usually not mindful that we have activated an unresolved memory from the past and are running disempowered patterns in the present. The anchor of awareness for this metaphor is a tool that helps us become aware enough to let go of the bone we're chomping on.

Imagine you are the captain of a big, beautiful 757 airplane. Go ahead: Put on your shiny, freshly pressed uniform and captain's hat.

Now, sense yourself in the captain's chair. All you can see is the runway in front of you getting smaller and smaller as you press the throttle and hear the engines roaring on takeoff.

As you glide smoothly into the bright blue sky, you look at the controls and notice there are two: autopilot and manual override. Now, as you are relaxing on your journey, the autopilot is guiding you. Do you notice and recognize when you begin to veer off course? Do you continue to stay on autopilot and veer into a raging storm of red-disempowered TEBS? See, hear, feel, and sense what it's like to be carried away by autopilot. Now, let yourself switch over to manual override. Feel how it is to be mindful in the moment so that you can override the autopilot and turn the plane toward the calm blue sky, returning to a grounded, centered state full of green-empowered TEBS.

Exploratory Questions

- In what realm or area of your life do you tend to be on autopilot, heading in the wrong direction? What does this look, sound, or feel like?
- When you are triggered, do you tend to remain in autopilot mode or intentionally switch to manual override? How are you able to notice and recognize when you begin to veer off course?
- What are the consequences to yourself and others when you are on autopilot and veer off course?
- Which strategies and tools have you chosen to use so you are able to easily switch over to manual override and return to a grounded and centered state? See it, hear it, feel it, sense it, be it!

_____

_____

_____

_____

_____

_____

Global Reflections

Refer to page 64 and answer each of the global reflection questions to give yourself the best chance of success for your efforts.

_____

_____

_____

_____

_____

_____

VAKing Tool 21: Hmm, That's Interesting: Challenge with a TFQ

This is the last VAKing tool I will offer you, for now. Of course, there are many more symbol, metaphor, and analogy tools, and they're scattered throughout the book. (I also encourage you to make up your own—it's really fun!) This final tool is an evaluative strategy that is one step in the M&M technique you'll learn about in chapter 6.

Imagine you are triggered and in a state of shift. You have come a long way and can now recognize and realize where you are, due to your mindful use of the neurological instruments in section 1 of this book. Once you are aware of your state, you can use your strategies and tools to get back below an NSI of 3. You cannot proceed until you are below an NSI of 3, which enables you to be present, nonjudgmental, centered, grounded, open, and flexible.

Now, imagine a little white cloud pop up above your head with a question mark embedded in it, just like you would see in a cartoon. This signals to you that it's high time to get curious. You say, "Hmm, that's interesting!" In fact, memorize this phrase, and as you say it, look up with curiosity. As you do so, place your index finger on the side of your face and say, "Hmm, that's interesting!" That's it!

So now that you've become inquisitive and have likely brought your NSI below a 3, you are ready to ask the challenge question: "What would I have had to believe about whomever or whatever triggered me in order for me to have the emotions and body sensations I was having?"

Once you get your answer, put it through the TFQ (true, false, or questionable) filter, which allows you to evaluate the belief you were unconsciously operating under when you got triggered. You'll find that the belief is rarely true. If it is questionable, place it in a toaster oven on a shelf in the back of your mind, and wait for it to go *bing!* and bring the answer up for you. By this, I mean that every situation must be evaluated on its own merits. If it is a real situation that requires immediate attention, then deal with it. Some of the time, it is something that will need time to percolate so the unconscious mind can come up with the answer by popping up into awareness, just like bread in a toaster oven.

Most of the time, you will answer false, if you are being honest and authentic with yourself. Then, you can flip your finger back at yourself and change the script from red to green; now, you have created the beginnings of a beautiful green-empowered neural pathway!

Exploratory Questions

- In what realm or area of your life have you chosen not to challenge your disempowered belief, causing yourself and others to suffer in some way? What does this look, sound, or feel like?

- Which tools have you practiced to recognize when you are triggered and in a state of shift so you can soothe your NSI back below a 3?
- Have you taken the time to memorize the phrase, "Hmm, that's interesting?" What does it look, sound, and feel like to use the phrase?
- To what situation can you now apply the challenge question: "What would I have had to believe about whomever or whatever triggered me in order for me to have the emotions and body sensations I was having?"
- What did you find when you followed through with the TFQ filter to evaluate whether the belief you were unconsciously operating under was true, false, or questionable?
- What was it like for you and someone else when you mindfully flipped your finger back at yourself and changed the script from red to green, creating the beginnings of a beautiful green-empowered neural pathway? See it, hear it, feel it, sense it, be it!

Global Reflections

Refer to page 64 and answer each of the global reflection questions to give yourself the best chance of success for your efforts.

_____

_____

_____

The Final Word

I've given you a ton of strategies and tools to use! I have no doubt that some will resonate and stick with you while others will feel less applicable or interesting. It may feel like drinking from the fire hose, but I encourage you to start small, perhaps focusing on one tool at a time before mixing and matching to create the combinations that work best for you. Over time, choose a handful and practice them repeatedly, with conscious competence, until you become unconsciously competent. Before you know it, you'll be VAKing It Up and choosing your chance for mindfulness without even having to think about it!

My hope is that when you sense even the slightest flicker of a trigger and activation of your inner world, you will be able to use your anchors of awareness to recognize and interrupt disempowered patterns. Remember, it is the steady and continual interruption of our patterns that helps us to mindfully manage our inner world and instill new, green TEBS. Sometimes, the most challenging part isn't the work itself—it's what it takes to notice our triggers in the moment and guide ourselves back to an NSI below 3. It truly only takes moments to reevaluate the meaning we've assigned, acquire valuable life learning lessons, and identify the empowered values you need to resource in order to become more resilient. Before you know it, you will be the captain of your own destiny, peacefully navigating the waters of the present moment rather than getting stuck in the riptides and gnarly currents of the past or future.

Busting the Boundaries of Your Triggered Protective Cycle

Owning our story can be hard,
but not nearly as difficult
as spending our lives running from it.

—Brené Brown

CHAPTER 5

Stimulus, Gap, Choice

*Between stimulus and response is a space.
In that space is our power to choose our
response. In our response lies our growth
and our freedom.*

−Viktor Frankl

For me, there's nothing quite as rewarding as knowing that the clients I've worked with have met the challenges of their lives not through reactivity but through the activation of their own inner MEL. This is the result of their doing the inner work to learn, stretch, heal, and grow.

One of my clients, Rose, recently shared her story of how her MEL showed up during a time when things could just as easily have gone the other way. It's such a wonderful account of how we develop unconscious competence through repetition of the strategies, tools, and techniques in this book.

Rose was in the middle of a conversation with her partner, Tom, who suffered from left-brainitis, which often created shock waves in their relationship. Tom was infected by the need to analyze, logicalize, rationalize, and strategize anything and everything, especially their relationship. As you can imagine, this was a point of contention for

Rose, who was learning to step into her MEL while holding a space of compassion and nonjudgment for Tom.

During their conversation, Rose became genuinely curious about Tom's need to be right all the time. She suspected that it pointed to a deep unresolved wound that had resulted in this rigid pattern. She gently prodded, "What is it about this situation that made you feel you did something that wasn't perfect?"

Tom scoffed at the question, but Rose persisted as respectfully as she could. "I want to go deeper and understand what makes up your inner world, what makes you tick."

"I don't know what you're talking about. I'm a problem solver, and you're the one who's the problem in this situation!" Tom shot back, arms across his chest.

This made Rose feel sad. She noticed that his eyes were vacant of any emotion. Tom even went so far as to add a hurtful jab: "I feel like I don't have a partner. You're more like a pet girlfriend, Rose!"

Rose knew that she could either get triggered and react, which meant they would both be stuck in their Triggered Protective Cycle, and the conversation would go south very quickly, or she could remain open and connected to her MEL values. She later told me, "I just kept asking him question after question, remaining as calm as I could in the situation. Somehow, it got to the point where he said, 'I'm not like you. I've worked through my drama and don't hold on to things.' I asked what he meant by that, because I wanted him to elaborate, to keep talking."

Rose eventually got Tom to open up. At some point, she asked him what the real feeling was behind all his anger. He became emotional and was almost in tears—something Rose had never seen, as Tom was not a very vulnerable person who had never allowed his vulnerability to be accessed. He admitted to her that he displayed anger to protect himself so that he'd never feel like a scared child again. Rose assured him that she loved him, and she even said, "Now that's the guy I wanted to talk to—not the bouncer! You're such a kind, sweet soul, and I just wanted to see it."

How did they get to that place? Rose used the anchors of awareness to hold her own space in the midst of a conflict that could have
ended in a knock-down, drag-out fight. Although Tom was dancing
with the *D*'s and acting like a bully, Rose told herself at the beginning,
"Whatever he's saying isn't about me, so I'm not going to take in the
darts he sends." She stuck with this strategy and, with some of the
techniques you'll learn about in volume 3, didn't let go until Tom
was able to go inside and downstairs and become aware of and share
his truth, when he disclosed a story about a much younger version of
himself that she'd never heard. In staying with her MEL, she opened a
door to flexibility, acceptance, and nonjudgment; and she also created
safety, certainty, and trust by choosing not to personalize his insults,
although he tested her multiple times! She was responsive rather than
reactive, curious rather than combative. She had learned over time to
step into her MEL, especially in hairy situations. Now, she'd finally
achieved a level of unconscious competence such that it had become
second nature.

Even though some choices we make are unconscious, we must
maintain the perspective that we *always* have a choice—just as Rose
did. We need to live by the perspective that we are *at cause* for anything
that happens within ourselves, while understanding that the external
world absolutely influences our system. Blaming others serves to dis-
empower us. If we do not adhere to the principle that we are at cause
for how we make sense of and assign meaning to our experiences,
then we will probably not believe that we can manage our meaning-
machine mind and change our patterns.

The first technique I share with clients, when they find themselves
stuck within the boundary of a problem, is to *lean into the boundary*
and begin to mindfully poke holes in it. Once you step outside the
boundary on multiple occasions, you start to realize and enhance your
personal power. This helps you to remain open to what is instead of
being trapped in what should be. Amazingly, this can help you to find
solutions where before you only found dead ends.

I use the concept of *stimulus, gap, choice* to help clients utilize the strategies and tools to recognize and interrupt the patterns inherent in the Triggered Protective Cycle. Through repetition, we can diminish the influence of our disempowered patterns. In this way, clients do the daily work of challenging the boundary of the Triggered Protective Cycle while also doing the deeper work of resolving their Core Identity Cycle, where the wounds originated. When practiced with consistency and congruency, results are achieved more rapidly and have a more empowering impact on their inner world.

The process of change is about learning and practicing the anchors of awareness that you learned in section 1 so you can be conscious of when you become triggered, identify your reactive body signals, and start to recognize and interrupt your disempowered patterns. You can then mindfully change the patterns and make an empowered choice. Thus, the process of firing and wiring new neural pathways for your healing and growth begins!

Stimulus, Gap, Choice:
Hmm, Which Way Do I Go?

A *stimulus* is sensory data that your nervous system can register in a nanosecond. You must consider the nature of the stimulus. If it evokes positive emotions, great! And we do not need to concern ourselves with this scenario. But, when the stimulus evokes a negative reaction in the nervous system, that is your inner world alerting you to danger, real or imagined.

The signal of the stimulus will be felt as a BSI before mindful recognition can register. The key to this technique is to listen to your body and recognize when it is sending you the cue to begin the strategy. This initial BSI is your EWAS. Remember to listen to these whispers from your body, not the chatter of your mind!

From the moment you associate with an unresolved wound, you may trigger and activate your nervous system. You receive the signals and feel unique body sensations. If you do not pay attention to them, you risk running the same patterns over and over. This may keep you stuck within the boundary of the Triggered Protective Cycle as your PODS take control. In this scenario, there is no gap between the stimulus and your reaction.

The *gap* is the time and space between the stimulus and your choice, and it can be either a *response* or *reaction*. This gap is usually measured in nanoseconds as you unconsciously process the sensory data, filter it through your references, and assign a meaning to it. The key to this step is using the anchors of awareness to mindfully increase the gap of time, so you give yourself a chance to reevaluate the meaning and make a new choice.

When you apply the anchors of awareness, you can attune to your body. You can recognize the EWAS and begin a process to grow your gap. When you grow your gap, you slow your nervous system down, quiet your mind, and reevaluate the meaning you previously assigned. This gives you the chance to make an empowered choice to change the meaning so that you can respond instead of offering a kneejerk reaction in the moment. And you can do this without any judgment! Once you have achieved a large enough gap multiple times, you may notice that you become less reactive, just as Rose did. This is because you have trained your unconscious mind to become unconsciously competent in a new pattern of assigning meaning to a specific context.

In chapter 3, I mentioned Tara Brach's acronym OWN (**o**bserve, **w**itness, and **n**arrate). When you can *observe* the shift in your nervous system, you can mindfully *witness* the pattern without integrating with it, and then you can *narrate* the story to yourself. Owning yourself, the way Rose did, is one way to increase the gap and make new empowered choices that connect you with your MEL.

Choice is the moment in your journey where you reach a fork in your river of life and must consciously or unconsciously choose how to make sense of something or someone. If the eyes are the window to the soul and your window is covered with dirt, the awareness and application of this technique will provide you with an opportunity to take *response-ability* to clean your window so that you may better attune to yourself and others and not veer off your mindful path.

There are two directions you can choose: You can take the *high road* or the *low road*. Each road has three distinct patterns. With each stimulus that activates your nervous system above a quake or shift, you must develop the habit of asking yourself the questions from section 1: "What would I have to believe in order to feel this way? Is it true, false, or questionable?"

The High Road:
The Mindful Way

When you choose to take the high road, you are mindful to stay within your zone of tolerance and maintain a wide gap between stimulus and choice. You assign empowered meanings to your experiences, follow patterns that move you toward others, and enjoy the positive outcomes that result from your choices. You unconsciously take the high road when you are living and being the MEL of your inner world.

If you are on this road, you can quickly come back to your center when you are triggered. When you assign self-empowered meanings, your TEBS reflect the following responsive patterns:

- Your *thoughts* are focused on others and are you- and we-centric.
- Your *emotions* are empathy and compassion.
- Your *behaviors* reflect how you respond and move toward others.
- Your *stories* reveal that you believe you are a participant and have a choice.

You also reflect the following characteristics:

- *openness* in how you evaluate the past, present, and future, without judgment;
- *curiosity* to ask questions and seek to understand before being understood;
- *reflectiveness* in considering multiple perspectives before making a choice; and

- *adaptability* in challenging situations by monitoring and modifying your patterns to self-soothe and stay centered and grounded.

The outcome of these patterns and characteristics will look like the following (which, not coincidentally, add up to the acronym SAFE):

- *Synergy* of your attuned communications, connections, and commitments
- *Acceptance* of yourself and others, and what was, is, and might be
- *Flexibility* around your meanings, beliefs, needs, evaluations, and responses
- *Empathy,* understanding, and compassion for yourself and others

The Low Road:
The Mindless Way

When you choose to take the low road—which most of us caught in the throes of our Triggered Protective Cycle do—your gap is narrow and you may easily stray outside the zone of tolerance and into rigidity or chaos. You assign a disempowered meaning to your experiences, follow patterns that move you away from or against others, and suffer the negative outcomes from believing that you do not have a choice or that you are a victim.

When you take the low road, you activate a Triggered Protective Cycle and erode your personal power. When you assign disempowered meanings, your TEBS reflect the following reactive patterns:

- Your *thoughts* are I-centric.
- Your *emotions* are anger, sadness, fear, shame, guilt, or hurt.
- Your *behaviors* reflect how you react and move away from or against others.
- Your *stories* reveal that you believe you are a victim with no choice.

You also reflect the following characteristics:

- *judgment* based on red rules that impact how you judge yourself, other people, places, and things, as well as the past, present and future;
- *defensiveness*, whereby you insist on being understood before you attempt to understand;
- *impulsivity* with your thoughts, emotions, behaviors, and choices, without consideration of the consequences; and
- *lack of openness* to challenging situations by refusing to monitor and modify your patterns to self-soothe and stay centered and grounded.

The outcome of these patterns and characteristics will look like the following (all of which mean you are absolutely not SAFE!):

- *Negativity* in your inner language of meanings, needs, beliefs, values, and judgments
- *Obstructions* in your relationship with self and others, caused by your rigid and chaotic TEBS
- *Turmoil* in your inner and outer world, resulting from your disempowered reactive information and energy flow
- *Conflict* within yourself and with others

Notice your own tendency when you get triggered. Do you take the low road of reactivity or the high road of responsiveness (and response-ability)? Keep in mind that there will be times when you will choose the low road, both consciously and unconsciously. Please don't be harsh with yourself when this happens, as every time you're triggered produces a new chance for choice. If and when you reach a fork in the road and realize that you do not really wish to take the low road, remember that you can always turn back with a two-step strut! You have the strategies and tools to course-correct, reevaluate the meaning you assigned, and make a mindful choice to flip red to green and take the high road instead.

Here's a song you can anchor in your head to help you choose the high road. (I imagine it being sung to the melody of Devo's "Whip It.")

When a trigger comes along, you must flip it!
Before the FID goes on too long, you must flip it!
When something's going wrong, you must flip it!
Now flip it, into shape.
Red to green—it's not too late.
Go forward. Don't associate.
Try to detect it—differentiate.
Now, flip it! Flip it good!

Exercise:
Identify Your Choice Patterns

Think of your chosen challenge from the introduction or recall a recent experience when a shift happened and you became reactive.

Stimulus

- What was the BSI indicating that a shift happened? (Note the FID of the sensations you felt.)
- Have you felt this particular sensation before? If so, under what circumstances?

_____

_____

_____

Gap

- How much time went by before you realized you were in a reactive space?
- What anchor of awareness can you use to OWN (**o**bserve, **w**itness, and **n**arrate) the state of your inner world in order to grow your gap the next time you are triggered in a similar way?

_____

_____

_____

Choice

- Review the following table and identify which road you usually travel depending on the context of the experience. Place an *X* next to the traits you displayed during this reactive event, then describe in detail how you showed up for each category.

TEBS	High Road	Low Road
Thoughts	___ We-centric	___ I-centric
Emotions	Empathy, ___ compassion	Anger, sadness, guilt, ___ fear, shame, hurt
Behavior	___ Moving toward	Moving away ___ or against
Stories	Participant, choice, ___ at cause	Victim, no choice, ___ at effect

_____

_____

_____

_____

_____

_____

How You Showed Up	High Road	Low Road
	__ Open	__ Judgmental
	__ Curious	__ Defensive
	__ Reflective	__ Impulsive
	__ Adaptive	__ Not open, closed off

_____

_____

_____

_____

_____

Outcome	High Road	Low Road
	__ Synergy	__ Negativity
	__ Acceptance	__ Obstruction
	__ Flexibility	__ Turmoil
	__ Empathy	__ Conflict

_____

_____

_____

_____

_____

_____

So far, you've learned a number of powerful strategies, tools, and techniques that will help you to become more aware of what lives in your unconscious so that you can make more conscious decisions. But please don't feel overwhelmed. Sometimes, you will feel tempted to judge yourself on how well you are "performing." But, as with Rose, it usually takes a period of trial and error until you can stand firmly in your MEL's shoes. You're on a journey, so don't judge it until you are farther along and closer to your desired destination. By the time you read volume 3 (which will address the experience of being in a committed love relationship), the landscape will look markedly different. You'll find yourself making sense of your life, including your deep-seated impulses and the experiences you've judged as "good" or "bad," through a totally different lens. By that time, you'll reevaluate "I" and "WE" so that you can make choices without judgment and honor both yourself and the person you love. All the tools you'll have picked up along the way will give you what you need to make the best decisions for yourself, however you define them.

The best living laboratory for the practice of NI is in a committed love relationship, or even with your children and family members. You have so many opportunities in these contexts to practice being mindful from moment to moment, and to utilize the strategies and tools you put in your NI toolbox to become unconsciously competent. This will give you the best chance of success to get to the next higher version of self.

Just be aware that the goal of this journey is clarity, and clarity evolves over time as you gain new experiences in different realms of your life. You don't have to force clarity to come; again, the way you perceive things will slowly but surely transform. When you have done the work, clarity appears of its own accord. So, give yourself permission to use the NI strategies, tools, and techniques in this book so that you can form new neural pathways that will aid you in making the clearest choices. The technique you're about to learn in chapter 6 will certainly help you on that journey.

The M&M Technique: Monitor and Modify Reactive Patterns

I free myself not by trying to be free, but by simply noticing how I am imprisoning myself in the very moment I am imprisoning myself.

—Rick Carson

As you've learned by now, the key to a happy life, in which you continue to learn, stretch, heal, and grow, is to accept absolute personal responsibility for your inner world and your choices. To do this, you must learn to monitor and modify your TEBS' reactive patterns that adversely impact the relationships you have with others and yourself. The first major technique, which I call "M&M," begins with noticing the EWAS in your body, which is the only way to properly increase and utilize the gap between a stimulus and a choice. Many of us haven't been trained to pay attention to our bodies so we can be absolutely clear what an NSI above a 3 or 4 feels like in a variety of contexts—allowing us to take meaningful steps to bring our NSI back down.

The M&M technique enables you to widen the gap enough so you can make responsive choices that lead to the high road of empowerment instead of reacting and making choices that hijack you and send you hurtling down the low road of disempowerment. The M&M technique is designed to help you engage a strategy within the gap when you get triggered and a shift happens. A shift-happens moment unconsciously links to an unresolved memory that is uniquely similar (in context, not content) to something occurring in the present. This will lead you to evaluate the present moment based on red-disempowered references constructed from the past. When this occurs, the energy and information stored in the Core Identity Cycle becomes activated in the present, outside of your awareness. Of course, the stimulus that's marked by the physiological shift in your body gives you an opportunity to become consciously aware that a shift happened. This is when it's time to mindfully recognize and interrupt the pattern by installing a new, green-empowered meaning in the moment. With repetition, you initiate a strategic process to retrain your brain, reconnect with your body, and rewire your nervous system to consciously change those old patterns that caused you and others so much suffering.

We've all experienced times when we get triggered and a shift happens—and we've certainly observed this in others. Usually, when this occurs, neither person has any idea what caused the trigger and why someone started to act out their own unique, special brand of weirdness! When these episodes occur, you hear people say things like, "What in the world happened to you? One minute you were fine, and then you went crazy?" or "We were having such a nice conversation, and then all of a sudden, you were gone—you just shut down and would not engage." This happens a lot in committed love relationships. When one or both partners experience a shift, they might start a negative tango that gets perpetuated and can escalate to a challenging and sometimes toxic cycle of conflict. Over time, this dysfunctional interaction will erode the foundation of safety, certainty, and trust in the space called "WE." For individuals, couples, families, and teams of people to stop negative cycles and show up in a flexible state, we must look in the mirror and hold ourselves accountable for the impact our past has on our present.

The Flow of M&M

Preparation

Before you learn any new technique, you must become proficient with the strategies and tools associated with the technique. In chapters 1 through 5, you've picked up a variety of instruments, strategies, and tools. Now, we will cover an example for how to apply these for the purpose of this technique. You will identify three challenges in the form of three past triggering experiences during which you became reactive; you'll use these as examples to practice the instruments, strategies, and tools in order to become proficient in the technique.

Application

Once you are aware of your challenges and understand how to use the instruments, strategies, and tools, you'll need to practice them—so when the time comes, you can mindfully apply them to achieve your desired outcome.

The application phase of this technique is designed to be used in the moment when a shift happens. The intention is for you to *recognize* your trigger signal and subsequently *recenter* your body to get your NSI below a 3 and begin to *refocus* your mind.

Evaluation

At some point, be it soon after you recenter your body or sometime further down the line, it will be time to evaluate what happened within you. In this section, you will continue to *refocus* your mind and *reframe* the disempowered belief that led to the trigger.

Re-Engage: Attune and Relate

If your reactive event caused a rupture in the bond between you and another, this is the time to *re-engage* the other by delivering a message that is honest, authentic, vulnerable, open, and truthful. (Volume 3 details something I call "the mindful discussion technique," which allows for healthy re-engagement.) Overall, during this process, you will share the truth of your inner world and begin to rebuild safety, certainty, and trust.

Repair: Show Up!

If you feel you have caused another pain and damaged a relationship, this is your opportunity to *repair* the bond by following the process and offering a sincere and genuine apology.

Preparation

Identify Your Challenge

1. <u>Triggering Experiences: When Shift Happened</u>

Think of three events (one of which, preferably, is recent) during which you know you got triggered, experienced a shift, and became reactive. In this book or your journal or digital device, describe when and how you felt this immediate change in your state. Include the month and year of each event. You will use all three events as you work through the exercises in this chapter.

- What happened in that moment? Who or what was the source of the trigger?
  - Was it something someone said or did, such as their facial expression or tone of voice?
  - Was it something you read (a book, article, or text message) or saw in a movie?
  - Was it a thought you had about something or a memory that came up out of nowhere?

_____

_____

_____

_____

_____

_____

- What was the physiological change? What did you feel in your body?
  - Was the body sensation in your groin, stomach, chest, heart, throat, or somewhere else?
  - What was the size, shape, and weight of the body sensation?
  - What was the color of the body sensation?
  - Was the body sensation intense or mild, cold or hot?
  - Was there any movement or vibration?
  - Did you feel constriction or expansion?

_____

_____

_____

_____

_____

_____

2. What's Your Modus Operandi (the Strategy for Your Reactive Patterns)?

What happened to you when you got triggered in the examples you wrote about? Did you become immobilized or energized? Were you emotionally stressed, distressed, anxious, angry, sad, shameful, or fearful? What was the physiological pattern of your reactivity?

Our patterns are displayed by the four pillars of our TEBS. Take some time to consider the reactive events you identified. Describe in detail what you remember about how each of these four pillars was activated when you got triggered and became reactive.

1. Thoughts
    - Were you focused on what you wanted or did not want?
    - Did your thoughts begin racing or did your mind freeze up?
    - What were the common language patterns (keywords and phrases) of your thoughts when you were in the reactive state?
    - Were your thoughts consumed with catastrophic language?

    _____

    _____

    _____

    _____

    _____

    _____

2. Emotions
    - Did you feel energized (like you were going to explode)?
    - Did you feel immobilized (like you were going to shut down and run away)?
    - What were your feelings (anger, sadness, fear, shame, guilt, or hurt)?
    - What were the distinguishing body sensations you experienced when you were triggered?
    - How old did you feel in that moment?

    _____

    _____

    _____

_____

_____

_____

3. Behaviors
   - What did you say or do that you know was reactive, inappropriate, and wish you had not?
   - Did you shut down and move away?
   - Did you shout out and move against?
   - Did you engage in dysfunctional behaviors, such as using spiteful verbal darts, passive-aggressive comments, minimizing, invalidating, getting even, criticizing, or lying?

_____

_____

_____

_____

_____

_____

4. Stories
   - Did you narrate a story in your head that was about defending, deflecting, debating, dismissing, and denying?
   - Was your story focused on accusing, blaming, or assuming something about someone or a particular situation?
   - Was the story based on a perception of your victimhood?
   - Was the story red and disempowered? In what ways did you give your power away when the shift happened?

_____

_____

_____

_____

_____

_____

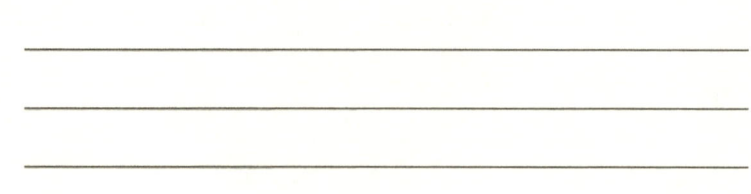

Application

<u>1. Recognize Your Signal: Wake Up!</u>
To begin the application steps, you will use a strategy that will help you wake up and recognize the signal emanating from your body. You will use the neurological instruments from chapter 1 to create your EWAS. You'll mindfully manufacture massive amounts of sensory data using AI and VAK It Up to create a metaphorical image that will then act as the wake-up call to get your prefrontal cortex—your mindful brain—to pay attention and take control.

I've developed four different tools to use the technique for waking up the conscious mind. Most people will resonate with one over the others. You can use these to begin or come up with your own original signal. No matter what you choose, remember to use a massive over-load of sensory data with AI and VAK It Up.

I call the first one *NORAD*, which stands for the North American Aerospace Defense Command. Imagine a fortified steel complex deep below a massive mountain, with alarms that will go off the second it detects an enemy's nuclear missile silo beginning to open. Sirens begin to boom, blinking colored lights go off, and a red "WARNING" sign flashes on a giant video screen in the background.

The next awareness tool is a *tornado siren*. Have you ever heard one before? It begins to blare out about five minutes before a tornado hits. Imagine standing on a street in a small town in Kansas, next to a pole with a giant red loudspeaker blasting the siren sound while you are staring at an F5 tornado heading toward you. Would you ignore the sound of the siren and the image of the tornado and do nothing to protect yourself?

The next one is for the older folks out there. When I was growing up, there was a TV show called *Lost in Space*. It was about the Robinson family and their journeys to new planets. In some of the episodes, the son, Will Robinson, would go exploring with the family's robot. Invariably, the robot would stop, and the lights around its head would twirl with different colored lights, and its arms would fling around wildly. Then the robot would say, "Danger, Will Robinson! Danger, Danger!"

The last choice is *the taser*. Imagine standing there and seeing a bright-red taser fully charged with a million volts heading your way, aimed right at your chest. You can see the squiggly lines representing the electricity and hear the sound of it loudly whirling toward you, about to shock your system.

Did you notice the VAKing I used to describe these tools? They are meant to alert your conscious mind to wake up and begin the process of overriding the unconscious danger signals being sent from your body, and to use massive amounts of sensory data.

Once you are aware that you are activated, triggered, or in a state of shift, you can begin using the following steps that involves strategies and tools that lower your NSI, the activation in your body. The common element here is breaking the state of activation by using mindfully manufactured sensory data with AI and VAK It Up.

Exercise: Wake Up!
Describe in vivid detail your wake-up strategies, choosing from the four strategies I just outlined and incorporating the tools you've already learned—or creating a different wake-up strategy that resonates with you.

_____

_____

_____

2.   Notice: How High Is My NSI?

When shift happens, your nervous system experiences a physiological reaction whereby energy is released and flows through or floods your body. You will come to recognize these sensations as your EWAS that you have shifted and are in a reactive state. In such a situation, ask yourself: "Which signal did I choose to use—or did I come up with one of my own?"

As you'll recall from volume 1, the NSI is a way for us to measure the intensity of activated energy in our body at any moment in time. The index is based on a 0–10 scale, 0 being no energetic reaction and 10 being the highest reaction. Let's say you had an experience whereby you got triggered. An NSI of 2 is a slight drift in your emotional state, where you might say, "I feel a little peeved." An NSI of 10 would describe a shift in which you felt overtaken by an uncontrollable rage or inconsolable crying.

In this step, we want to develop a strategy using the neurological instruments of AI and VAK It Up. Think of a cartoon character, a character from a movie, or someone you know from the past who makes you chuckle whenever they come to mind. You want to make sure this image is light, positive, and humorous. Now, with AI, VAK It Up, and nonverbal signals, embellish it and make it as silly, goofy, and outrageous as possible. You'll want to create a three- to five-second mini movie of this character or person and run it through your mind quickly. Keeping the image in mind, ask, "How high is my NSI?" Notice the score that comes into your awareness. See it as a giant red pulsating number. It is imperative for you to mindfully manufacture massive sensory data and see this scene in bright vivid colors, hear it loud and clear, and feel the humorous emotions intensely.

Exercise: How High is My NSI?

Describe in vivid detail the humorous scene you just developed, incorporating the neurological instruments when you ask, "How high is my NSI?"

_____

_____

_____

3. Pause: I Have Cause for a Pause

Immediately after you ask "How high is my NSI?" say, "I have cause for a pause." You can use the same scene and character you just used, or you can create a new one. Either way, make sure you apply the neurological instruments appropriately to match the intention of the phrase. This step will continue the process of breaking your state and interrupting your reactive neuronal firing patterns. Make sure you say "I have cause for a pause" with a positive, humorous emotional state to send a powerful signal from your conscious mind to your unconscious mind that you really *do* need to pause the reaction. An idea I share with clients is to picture a giant red stop sign or a set of railroad crossing bars moving side to side in a goofy way.

Exercise: I Have Cause for a Pause

Describe in vivid detail the pause scene you developed, incorporating the neurological instruments when you say, "I have cause for a pause."

_____

_____

_____

4. Exhale: Breathe and Release the Energy

Once you pause, the next step is to begin the process of soothing your nervous system. The best way to accomplish this is by using your breath. Begin by taking at least three to five deep 4-6-8 intentional breaths and say the following phrase to yourself: "Breathe and release the energy." Inhale deeply into your abdomen and exhale with intention, heaving a sigh of relief on your exhale: "Ahhhhhh." See, hear, feel, and sense the energy exiting your mouth, dispersing into the air, and most importantly, disappearing into the distance. Use the John Coffey exercise or the surfing method from section 2 to mindfully exhale some of the reactive energy from your body and further lower your NSI.

Along with the breath and saying the phrase, use AI and VAK It Up and create a scene in nature that is the most relaxing place in the world. It could be on a beach, on a boat, in the mountains, under a waterfall, in the forest, or anywhere else you associate with relaxation. What do you see, hear, and feel? Create a vivid, detailed mini movie in your mind.

The most important part of this step is to recognize the energy in your body and begin to feel safe with it. Your body may feel like it is signaling that you are in danger in some way, and your NSI might be a 6 or higher. Use this time to allow your conscious mind to send a message that you are safe as you become comfortable with that which was previously uncomfortable. Try your best to stay with the emotions and body sensations until they begin to subside; do this without judgment until you soothe your nervous system below an NSI of 3. This is how you begin to reconnect your mind, emotions, and body. If you have time, you can lead yourself in a guided visual meditation while breathing as you incorporate the next step.

Exercise: Breathe and Release the Energy
Describe in vivid detail the scene you just developed, incorporating the neurological instruments when you say, "Breathe and release the energy."

_____

_____

_____

5. Move: Shake It Out!
It is important to move your body in some way to shake off the energy, in much the same way an animal does after an intense encounter. If

you don't, the energy may stay trapped in your body. Use the neurological instruments and see, hear, and feel the energy dropping off and away from your body. Almost as if you were a dog shaking off water, see, hear, feel, and sense the energy leaving all parts of your body, dispersing into the air, and most importantly, disappearing into the distance.

Exercise: Shake It Out!
Describe in vivid detail the shake-it-out scene you developed, incorporating the neurological instruments when you shake off the energy.

_____

_____

_____

6. Awareness: Is This About Then or Now?

This particular step incorporates two concepts that I refer to as *actuality scales* that help us measure the actuality of the experience we are having. In other words, are you experiencing something that is true and real, or is it a reference from the past you have consciously or unconsciously associated with?

Disconnection Principle

I used to play the high striker at the yearly county fair (the one where you take a sledgehammer, hit the base at the bottom of the tower, and see if you can get the bell at the top to go off). Imagine two high strikers standing side by side: The one on the left has a green sign above it that says "Reality." The one on the right has a red sign above it that says "Reactivity." Both are marked 0 to 10, with 10 at the very top. A 10 on the left tower represents a *realistic* state of absolute direness, such as the sense that someone you love very much has just died. The tower on the right represents a state of reactivity where 10 is "thermonuclear" (chaos) or "arctic ice" (rigidity).

Considering the tower on the right, what is the rating you would give to the body sensation or emotional intensity you feel in your body? Now, consider the tower on the left. Where does the *reality* of the situation rank? Referring to the green sign on the left tower and comparing your perception of what triggered you to how you felt when someone you love just died will put everything into a proper perspective.

Let's compare the two scores. If you rated the situation a 1 or 2 in reality and your reactivity score was above a 6, that is the essence of a disconnection. This would indicate that you are linking something from the past to the present and being reactive. If you rated the situation a 5 and your reaction is a 7, it would indicate you are connected to the actuality and responding appropriately.

24-Hour Rule

Ask yourself the following question: "Will this situation, whatever it is that is triggering me, have a real impact on the quality of my life, my family's life, or my professional life in the next twenty-four hours?" If you answer no, it's a confirmation of the disconnection principle and suggests you are not responding to what is actually happening but reacting to something linked to the past.

Exercise: Is This About Then or Now?

Rate your score for each of the two actuality scales described in the disconnection principle.

_____

_____

_____

7. Challenge: Hmm, That's Interesting

This step enables you to determine whether you choose to defend and blame or own and change. Asking the challenge question helps you reevaluate your story and accept ownership. It allows you to see the world differently, to step outside of your comfort zone, and stretch past resistance. The ability to look in the mirror and examine your pattern of meaning evaluation leads to increased flexibility.

The challenge question is: "What would I have to believe in order to feel this way?" In other words, what would you have to believe about the situation, thought, person, place, or thing that triggered you and manifested the shift in emotional energy and body sensation in order for you to feel the way you felt at that time? For example, would you have to believe a person had malicious intent when they did/did not or said/did not say something to you? Would you have to believe that you were a victim in some way?

Next, put this through the TFQ filter: "Is this **true**, **false**, or **questionable**?" If it is true, then it is what it is. If false, it indicates you need to reevaluate the meaning you assigned. If questionable, I encourage you to consider various perspectives so you can learn and grow from the experience.

Exercise: Hmm, That's Interesting
Answer the challenge question: "What would I have to believe in order to feel this way?" After you have answered the question, put it through the TFQ filter and describe your answer. Whatever the result, approach it with curiosity and openness, which will help you learn and grow from the experience.

_____

_____

_____

8. Locate: Identify Your BSI

This last step is to be completed after you've had a chance to recenter your body. It is important to identify your primary BSI for future use with other exercises in the Re-Claiming Process.

If you tend to be chaotic when you are triggered, you may feel energized. If you tend to be rigid, you may feel immobilized. You may experience a tingling sensation in your chest or feel heat emanating from your heart region. Do you sense a sickening feeling in the pit of your stomach or a sensation of pressure building in your throat? Do you experience a feeling in your chest like it is about to collapse under the weight of pressure, or sense a sinking feeling in your stomach? Do you feel an energy jolt in your fingers that makes it feel like you are plugged into an electrical socket?

Refer to the reactive events you described in the Preparation section (page 176). Try the best you can to allow your unconscious mind to take you back to that moment and sense the body sensations you felt at that time. What was the location, size, shape, feel, sound, smell, color, temperature, texture, weight, pressure, movement, and vibration of the reactive energy?

Exercise: Identify Your BSI

Describe your reactive BSI in vivid detail, focusing on all aspects of the reactive body sensation. Then assign these inner body feelings or outer body sensations a name. If you can name it, you can tame it!

_____

_____

_____

Evaluation

Refocus Your Mind

This process enables you to flip your finger to yourself before you get a flipped finger pointing at you! Once you have completed the application steps, you should have lowered your NSI below a 3 and realized that your reaction was about something internal rather than external. The evaluation steps can be accomplished soon after you complete the application steps or anytime later that's right for you. The goals are for you to be deliberate and mindful as you work through the steps to change the disempowered meaning and belief that sparked your trigger. When you mindfully choose to change a disempowered belief multiple times, you will begin to flip your red references to green. This is the ultimate goal of the M&M technique.

1. Observe: Lay like OCRA

OCRA is the acronym that denotes the qualities of being in a flexible state:

- **O**pen to evaluate the past, present, and future without judgment
- **C**urious to ask questions and seek to understand before being understood
- **R**eflective to take time to consider multiple perspectives before making a decision
- **A**daptive with challenging situations by monitoring and modifying your thoughts, emotions, and behaviors to self-soothe, stay centered, and remain in flow

After you were triggered, you ideally recentered your body, lowered your NSI, and began to refocus your mind. Now, take some time to reflect. Be mindful of your body sensations when you were triggered. Notice but do not engage the reactive thoughts you had at that time. Reflect on the cacophony of your upstairs commentators, as well as the key words and phrases that were part of the narrative you were telling yourself in that moment. With intention, imagine yourself taking two steps back and observing your inner dialogue—the story you were telling yourself in your mind. When you can differentiate and not integrate with the story, you will be flexible enough to complete this step. As you examine your reactive experience, ask yourself the following questions.

- How old did this feeling feel?
- How old did I feel in that moment?
- How old was I acting in that moment?"
- Was I thinking and acting like a child or reptile?

_____

_____

_____

When you get triggered, you may regress back to an earlier age that's associated with the NUB in your Core Identity Cycle. Becoming aware of the age of this feeling will assist you as you move forward in the Re-Claiming Process.

Exercise: Observe: Lay Like OCRA
Answer the four questions below.

- Open: Did I evaluate the person, situation, or event in the present moment without judgment? If not, what was the judgment I had?

_____

_____

_____

- Curious: Did I ask inquisitive questions to understand before being understood? If not, what questions could I have asked to make it about the other and not myself?

_____

_____

_____

- Reflective: Did I take the time to think about different perspectives before making an impulsive choice? If not, what new perspectives could I have considered?

_____

_____

_____

- Adaptive: Did I monitor and modify my thoughts and emotions to self-soothe, stay centered, and remain flexible? If not, what could I have done to take that time to do so?

_____

_____

_____

2. Judgments: What's the Hook?

To reframe the meaning and desensitize the trigger, you must discover the triggering keywords and phrases within the story you are telling yourself that have caused a shift in the first place.

AEOs (agendas, expectations, and obligations) act as rules you create to determine whether a belief is true or false. You assign an AEO rule for what has to happen or not happen for a belief to be true or false; this usually happens unconsciously. AEO rules come in green and red. A green rule is based on mindful boundaries about your values. Green rules are healthy and functional, based on what you will and will not accept. A red AEO rule is about trying to control other people, situations, and things. Red rules are not healthy and are dysfunctional. When a red rule is broken, you feel pain in some way. You act as your own supreme court chief justice by passing down a verdict. Next, you call out your special forces to defend your story to the bitter end, not caring about other people's feelings or consequences.

There are three steps to assigning judgments you use to construct your disempowered stories. First is the trigger that hooks when a red AEO rule is broken; then you pass a sentence with your DABA (denial, accusation, blame, assumption) verdicts; and finally, you defend your story with your JERC (**j**ustifying, **e**xcusing, **r**ationalizing, **c**ajoling) defenses.

Exercise: Judgments: What's the Hook?
Be honest, authentic, vulnerable, open, and real as you write out the rules, verdicts, and defenses you used. Recognize the negative patterns you engaged in when you became reactive.

AEO Rules: Agendas, Expectations, Obligations
- Did you create any **a**gendas to lie, deceive, manipulate, or betray?
- Were you imposing any **e**xpectations to get, receive, take, or steal something?
- What **o**bligations did you attach to yourself, other people, places, and things in order to impact the outcome in your favor?
- Did you have any AEOs about what should have been, what should be now, or what could have been?

_____

_____

_____

DABA Verdicts: Denial, Accusations, Blame, Assumptions
- Were you in **d**enial about taking responsibility for the outcome of a situation?
- Did you make any **a**ccusations toward people, places, or things, based on fact or fiction?
- Whom or what did you **b**lame and point a finger at for bringing about the situation?
- Did you **a**ssume someone else's feelings, intentions, or thoughts?

_____

_____

_____

JERC Defenses: Justifying, Excusing, Rationalizing, Cajoling
- How did you justify your story, and what truths were you trying to hide from?
- What excuses did you make for your decisions to protect your story?
- How did you rationalize your story to validate whatever red AEO rule was broken?
- Whom or what were you cajoling to protect your DABA verdicts?

_____

_____

_____

3. Examine: Connect the Dots

It is now time to understand the process your nervous system went through that led to the activation. *Connect the dots* is a series of three questions that help you understand how you got to the point of having your brain believe you were in danger in some way. This is the fastest conversation you will ever have with yourself.

The first question is: "What is uniquely familiar about this situation?" Consider this from a global perspective—that is, think about the context without comparing content, data points, or actual events to previous experiences. Think back to previous INEs and see if you can discover the red reference you used in that event. Was it a verbal or nonverbal signal that triggered you? Was it something you saw, heard, or felt? Was it a pattern of speech, a facial expression, body language, or an energy you sensed? Was it a pattern of behavior you perceived, such as a passive-aggressive comment, a putdown, or a zinger?

The second question is: "What does this mean to me, about me, or for me?" This question has three possible answers.

1. Something is happening to me (usually links with an external fear belief).

2. Something happening is about me (usually links with an internal shame belief).

3. Something is happening for me (usually means you have a neural pathway that allows you to mindfully evaluate the situation for your learning and growth).

The third question is: "Am I safe or in danger?" Typically, the way you answered the first two questions will lead to the answer for the final question.

Exercise: Connect the Dots

Answer the three questions using the reactive events from step 1 (identify your challenge).

1. What triggered me: "What is uniquely familiar about this situation?"

2. How I assigned a meaning: "What does this mean to me, about me, or for me?"

3. Activation: "Am I safe or in danger?"

_____

_____

_____

Reframe Your Belief

The meaning you assign to an event or experience, and the subsequent belief you create, is and always will be your choice! Once you understand how you were linking with the past, the next step involves reframing your perspective of the present. To accomplish this, ask yourself insightful questions and be open and curious about how you can view this situation from a different, green-empowered perspective. If the trigger involves another person, try to put yourself in their shoes, see the world through their eyes, and understand where they are coming from. The ability to consider multiple perspectives and consciously choose new, empowered meanings is the basis for changing negative, disempowered patterns.

4. Questions: Stretch and Grow

This step in reframing your belief begins with asking neurological growth questions to help you stretch past resistance and grow into the next highest version of yourself. When you ask empowering questions based on "what" rather than "why," you are focused on the solution, which will enable you to grow. Here, you have a vital opportunity to flip the script, lock in your learnings, and fill up on your own empowered values.

Exercise: Stretch and Grow
Answer the following questions in detail.

- **Meaning:** What was the red-disempowered meaning I assigned? What green-empowered meaning can I choose to reframe my perception—how I made sense of my experience—so it serves to inspire me to move forward and help me focus on what I want in order to grow into the next highest version of myself?

_____

_____

_____

- **Learnings:** What life learning lessons am I supposed to acquire from this living laboratory of life experience that is trying to teach me something? What are the pearls of wisdom and knowledge I can gain from this experience?

_____

_____

_____

- **Values:** What are the empowered values I need to resource to become more resilient? What values did I need at that time but did not have access to that I can focus on resourcing so I will be prepared to mindfully employ my strategies and tools?

---

5. Choices: Opportunity for Growth

Once you have reframed the meaning, acquired your lessons, and resourced the values that allow you to be more flexible and resilient, it is time to explore this situation from three different perspectives. The three perspectives will help you choose new green-empowered meanings to replace the old red-disempowered meanings that caused your shift to happen.

Exercise: Opportunity for Growth

Reexamine your choice from the following three perspectives. What new choices could you make that will lead you to stretch and grow?

- **I:** With the insight you have gained, how are you currently looking at this situation through your mind's eye? What self-empowered meaning do you consciously choose to adopt at this moment?

- **You:** Place yourself in the other person's shoes and see the world through their eyes. How do they see it? Try the best you can to understand their perspective, validate their meaning, and empathize with how the situation made them feel.

_____

_____

_____

- **We:** In this perspective, I want you to be an objective observer from a distance. Stretch yourself and think outside the box. Float up to 18,000 feet and take a big-picture view that lets you see the situation from all angles. Develop a higher-level meaning that is a win-win for all.

_____

_____

_____

6. Decision: Step Up!

It is now time to decide and write out your new green-empowered belief regarding the triggering event you have been working through. Take the empowering keywords and phrases from steps 4 (stretch and grow) and 5 (opportunity for growth) that resonate with you the most and combine them to write your new beliefs. You will create an incantation for each new belief. An incantation can be written in two ways: You can write out a short paragraph using the keywords and phrases that describe your new belief, or you can create a rhyming poem you can easily remember and recite whenever necessary.

Exercise: Step Up!

Write out your new green-empowered belief for each of the events; you will be using this for the next step.

_____

_____

_____

7. Install: Fire and Wire!

To obtain and sustain the change you seek, you must complete this final step. It is imperative that you create a daily routine to read, visualize, and verbalize your new belief three times a day for thirty-three days. This is where you'll use all your discipline and resourcefulness to challenge yourself to take the last step in becoming your higher self. You have put in so much hard work to get to this point, you can't stop now!

I suggest that you put your incantations in the Notes app on your phone or write them on an index card and carry them around with you. You can write as many incantations as you desire. Write out a few of them on index cards or sticky notes to leave in strategic places as a reminder to send a signal to your unconscious mind and reprogram your MAP (your **m**eaning **a**ssigning **p**attern, which you learned about in volume 1). Use the neurological instruments as you read your incantations and mindfully manufacture massive amounts of sensory data. VAK It Up by seeing a detailed image that represents the meaning of the incantation. Hear yourself saying the words and feel the energy of the emotions evoked. Ensure that your facial expressions match the intention of the incantation. Use a speech pattern that matches the intention and do the same with your body movements. Breathe into the moment and raise your energy by doing all of this with a high positive NSI. Most important, make sure that as you engage your incantation you do so with a positive, elevated peak emotional state, which will enable you to anchor in the new empowered energy. If you are having difficulty anchoring a positive state, use AI to recall or fabricate an amazing experience that allows you to easily step into joyful, positive emotions.

Exercise: Fire and Wire!

Describe the daily routine you will employ to fire and wire your new green-empowered belief. How will you use the neurological instruments as you recite each of your incantations?

_____

_____

_____

Re-Engage:
Attune and Relate

Now that you've completed all the M&M steps, you can take action congruent with your new choice. The ability to show up in a centered, responsive state and to re-engage with someone or something after you have been triggered will be the most important indicator of your growth and the health of your relationships.

Begin by doing a self-check. How high is your NSI? Make sure it is below a 3 before you respond to the other person. In volume 3, you will learn more about the mindful discussion technique, which is an extraordinary practice for re-engagement. For our purposes here, this is a preview: In a discussion there are two people, a sender and a receiver of energy and information. Depending on the context of the situation and which role you need to step into, the ultimate objective for this technique is to establish rapport with another's unconscious mind to achieve two goals. The first is to repair the rupture in the primal attachment bonds of safety, certainty, and trust. The second is for the other person's unconscious mind to be able to answer the primary attachment question "Are you there for me, the way I need you, when I need you the most?" with a yes.

Repair:
Show Up!

If you have ruptured a relationship, it is your responsibility to repair it. When we are triggered, we might end up damaging the connection with ourselves or others, which means we need to take ownership of these decisions as soon as possible. This is the time to express empathy, compassion, and understanding; to offer a message of remorse, regret, and apology in a sincere and genuine manner.

Whom have your reactive patterns been damaging? (Remember, this might not be solely another person; it could be you.) Have you violated someone's primal attachment needs of safety, certainty, and trust and caused emotional distress, disappointment, frustration, or pain? Perhaps there were times when you knew you didn't show up for someone the way they needed you when they needed you the most. Or maybe there was a time when you did not keep your promises or commitments, and you now need to acknowledge the effect this has had on others.

Here are four steps to a successful apology (please note that by *successful*, I am not referring to the other person's response, but to your approach).

1. In an honest, sincere, and genuine manner, admit and unconditionally own what you did/said or did not do/say.
2. Explain in detail why what you did/said or did not do/say was wrong; express empathy as you do so.
3. Present a new empowered perspective about the situation by thinking about what you learned from the situation and using this lesson to act in more constructive ways in the future.
4. Describe in detail an action plan or strategy to demonstrate that this will not happen again and then follow through with your actions and words.

Here are a few things to remember when you are issuing an apology.

- There can be no qualifications—that means zero JERC moves of justifications, excuses, rationalizations, or cajoling!
- There can be no use of the word *but*.
- There can be no DABA verdicts of denying, accusing, blaming, or making assumptions about others.
- Don't dance with the deadly *D*'s: denying, defending, deflecting, debating, or dismissing.
- You must be perceived as sincere, genuine, and authentic. Say it like you mean it, and be sure that your facial expressions, body language, and words are aligned with your intended meaning.

When people are repairing a rupture, it's important to recognize that words are letters strung together to state the intention of potential promises. But alone, they are not enough. Actions are behaviors we see, hear, and feel that reflect and actualize the reality of these promises. The M&M technique is a wonderful way to remind ourselves that an integral part of living a green-empowered life is taking absolute responsibility for our impact on the outer world. Then we can ensure our intentions are aligned with the impact we have as well as with the degree of satisfaction we experience in all relationships—including the one with self. Remember, we always have a choice! We can stay stuck in old, disempowered patterns, or we can do the work to learn, stretch, heal, and grow!

Reveal, Release, and Resolve Your Core Identity Cycle

*The cave you fear to enter
holds the treasure you seek.*

–Joseph Campbell

CHAPTER 7

Welcome to
the Re-Claiming Process

It's not what happens to you—
it's what happens within you.

–Glenn S. Cohen

In section 1, you learned about the neurological instruments. You also practiced and are now, hopefully, ready to apply the mindfulness strategies and VAKing tools (which comprise your anchors of awareness) to *recognize* and *interrupt* disempowered patterns. In section 2, you used stimulus, gap, choice and the M&M technique to install new empowered patterns with mindful attention and repetition and bust the boundaries of your Triggered Protective Cycle—which will be especially helpful as you work to strengthen your relationships with self and others.

Section 3 focuses on the Core Identity Cycle that is unresolved and has become the potent fuel that activates your Triggered Protective Cycle. This is your introduction to the Re-Claiming Process.

Some of my clients often just want to focus on the present and on busting the boundaries of their Triggered Protective Cycle, which we covered in the first two sections of the book. You can work on using the NI strategies and tools to notice your stimulus, increase the gap, and learn to be mindful of your chance for choice. You can use the M&M technique to monitor and modify reactive patterns. You can associate with and activate your MEL to guide you to make choices that honor yourself and others. You can, through consistent repetition, learn how to mindfully change your language and start flipping your red references to green. All of this will help decrease the influence your PODS have in the present. However, you need to be mindful that any unresolved aspects inside you may unduly influence your nervous system in the future.

Doing the deeper inner work of revealing, releasing, and resolving your Core Identity Cycle is the ultimate key to healing any fractures in your inner world. This section of the book covers the aspects of the Re-Claiming Process that focus on the past to heal whatever is unresolved and help you reclaim your original, innate wholeness. We never know how our past impacts our present until we unpack the past in the present. The ultimate outcome for the Re-Claiming process is when you can truly quiet your mind, relax your body, and sense peace in your soul as you show up consistently and congruently as the MEL of your own inner world.

When you work with the Re-Claiming Process, you work with all three aspects of your inner world. You begin by associating with and activating your MEL. You need this highest aspect of self to show up to guide the other aspects via the multiple steps of the Re-Claiming Process. You then meet and greet your PODS to identify the ones who are most protective of your inner world (and who are likely responsible for hijacking your relationships with self and others). Then, you identify and locate your NUBs, and with all three aspects of your inner world together at last, you perform neurological surgery on yourself. The Re-Claiming Process is truly an amazing inner world healing experience!

Sometimes, my wonderful left brain–dominant clients encounter challenges when working on the aspect of the process that involves

SIMEs, which are guided meditations that have a strategic intention dependent on the step of the process you are working on. When you work with your inner world, it is critical to understand that you must let go of the present in order to let go of the past. You have to give yourself permission to believe in the make-believe and suspend all judging, analyzing, logicalizing, rationalizing, or strategizing, all of which are meant to help you make sense of something. The unconscious mind of your inner world has no concept of time or space and is not logical, rational, or linear. In fact, it has many minds of its own!

Throughout any journeys you take, make sure you use AI and VAK It Up. In addition, see what you see, hear what you hear, feel what you feel, sense what you sense, and be present in the experience in that present moment. There is no wrong or right way to feel, think, or be. I encourage you to go into the experience with the innocence of a child who is enchanted by their own inner world. Just allow yourself to be who you are, where you are, and when you are, without judgment. Know that you can listen and hear the messages, insights, and wisdom of your unconscious mind—as so many wise men and women have done through the ages when they dared to truly know themselves. You can trust and allow your unconscious mind to go where it wants to go and do what it needs to do, knowing that you will reap the benefits in your conscious waking life.

During the SIME inductions that you'll get a chance to listen to when you scan the QR codes in chapter 12, take heed that, if your wandering mind becomes distracted by your inner commentators at any time, you can simply notice them chattering about this, that, or the other—then with loving kindness, bring your intention and attention back to my voice, your breath, and your body in the present moment, opening your unconscious mind to new thoughts, new ideas, and new experiences.

There are nine steps involved in the Re-Claiming Process. This chapter explains step 1. In chapters 8 through 10, you will work on three exercises for step 1. The first is to associate with and activate your MEL; the second is to read a fable I created that is a metaphor for the three aspects of your inner world (you'll recognize it from volume 1, although this version is more interactive); the third helps you identify your top five PODS based on a comprehensive inventory I have created over the years. (You'll also remember this exercise from volume 1, although I always recommend a refresher from time to time). Chapter 11 covers step 2, part 1 and begins your education on SIMEs.

Chapter 12 will offer details about the rest of the steps. You'll be given QR codes for step 2 (parts 1 and 2) and step 3 (parts 1, 2, and 3). From there, you will partake in the rest of the Re-Claiming Process in a format of your choice (one-on-one coaching, a live weekend format, or a virtual weekly workshop format). You will be able to find more information about this on my website, www.centerforni.com. I saved the rest of the Re-Claiming Process for a more "experiential" and interactive format because I recognize the potency of diving into work like this. I was grateful to have had many guides steward me through transformative processes, and the Re-Claiming Process is no different. You will see the most benefits with clear and measured guidance that will help you titrate and integrate everything you've learned so far.

Step 1:
Exploring Your Unlimited Inner World

I enthusiastically welcome you to step 1 of the Re-Claiming Process! I hope you feel inspired and passionate to continue healing your past, clarifying your present, and growing into the next highest version of yourself.

Before you begin any journey, you need to plan and prepare for what is to come. Step 1 is the preparation phase of this journey and will help you gain clarity and lay the groundwork for the inner work you are about to engage in. Think of it as your time to pack your suitcase with all the essentials of your learning so that you can make the most of the journey, which is just as vital as the destination.

We begin with a review of the three aspects of your inner world:

1. **MEL:** The **m**indful **e**mpowered **l**eader. This is the highest version of self that lives by and honors your most important values. It is also the aspect of self that represents the true nature of your heart and soul. It shows up as HAVOR (**h**onest, **a**uthentic, **v**ulnerable, **o**pen, and **r**eal) with yourself and others.

2. **NUBs:** You already know that we all have a Core Identity Cycle that contains **n**eurological **u**nresolved **b**undles. These inner children and wounded adults are stuck, frozen in time in your inner world. Your NUBs contain the painful emotions and disempowered beliefs that become activated by your perception of the present, which unconsciously associates with the past.

3. **PODS:** Your **p**ersonalities of **o**ffensive and **d**efensive **s**trategies are the protective patterns you created at some point in life after a NUB was formed. Your PODS' primary purpose is to guard your vulnerable NUBs from being triggered and reexperiencing the painful emotions and activating the disempowered beliefs caused by an INE (**i**mpactful **n**eurological **e**xperience). PODS are the aspects of self that usually cause negativity, obstruction, turmoil, and conflict in your inner and outer worlds.

A Three-Part Exercise for Inner Exploration

Each part of step 1 builds on the next. You will work on these three exercises concurrently.

- *Part 1 Exercise: Install Your Mindful Empowered Values*—You will apply a daily plan to install your MEL values. You will have the opportunity to write about and describe the vision you have for your future self.

- *Part 2 Exercise: Legend of Cenneuint*—This is the fable that was included in volume 1. The difference this time is that you will read the fable and answer the questions for a deeper exploration of your inner world.

- *Part 3 Exercise: Meet and Greet Your PODS*—This is the same exercise that you encountered at the end of volume 1. Over time, your dominant PODS shift, as others will transform and experience an empowered purpose. You will identify your PODS and their favorite weapons of choice, then begin the process of connecting with them as your MEL.

Review of the Neurological Instruments

We will be using all the neurological instruments you learned in chapter 1. The following are the three most important instruments.

- **AI:** Active imagination is the most important instrument you will use to conduct neurological surgery on yourself. This requires you to willingly suspend disbelief and give yourself permission to believe in the make-believe.
- **VAK It Up!** You will use your visual, auditory, and kinesthetic senses to see, hear, feel, sense, and be it! You are a sensory data machine programmed by external and internal input throughout your life. When you mindfully VAK It Up, you will intentionally manufacture massive amounts of sensory data within your system to change the programming codes of your unconscious mind.
- **Nonverbals:** These are the megaphone of the unconscious mind. When you are on a journey, it is important to ensure that your nonverbals are congruent with the VAKed-up scene in your AI. This allows your unconscious mind to actualize that which your conscious mind chooses to believe.

When applied, the exploratory exercises will lead you to carve out new, empowered neural pathways that will help you become more flexible in navigating the challenging interactions and contexts of your life. You may experience some resistance as you work through these exercises. The cacophony of your inner commentators may chirp negative messages like, "This is stupid," "It will never work," "You're too tired, too busy, too far gone." You might even feel familiar emotions of anger, sadness, fear, shame, guilt, hurt, or hopelessness.

This is all normal and not a reason for despair or paralysis. Healing and growth will only happen when you make a conscious choice to apply the strategies, tools, and techniques with consistency and commitment over time. Breaking through resistance means surrendering to the present and accepting all aspects of yourself, free of judgment. You humbly acknowledge your novice status on this journey and let go of any disempowered judgments you may have placed on yourself and others. In fact, it can often be powerful to engage with a beginner's mind, as if you were doing something for the first time. People often feel pressured to know everything from the get-go, although this isn't a realistic expectation. When you approach something as if you don't know "how" to do it, you can give yourself permission, grace, and time to learn how. As you continue doing it over and over, you become comfortable with that which was once uncomfortable.

Over time, you will start to form new green-empowered references. Essentially, you will rewire your mind and re-prime your mirror neurons to deduce that you are safe when you are safe. If you mindfully manage your TEA (instead of spilling it!), it doesn't matter how emotionally fit you are when you start this journey. You can decide to raise your standards for yourself.

When I see my clients take this critical step, I often notice an incredible ripple effect: The more they associate with their MEL values and reclaim their inner world, the more those values start to positively influence the many realms of their lives.

These exercises constitute the inner work that will help you continue the process of changing your disempowered patterns. It is imperative that you engage these as instructed so that you can fire and wire in new patterns. Do the best you can to set a routine for the time of day you engage in these exercises. Remember, there is no wrong or right way to do them. Be flexible. It's not black and white. Try the best you can and do the best you can. As always, you get out what you put in. As always, it's your choice. You can do as little or as much as you desire. You will get something out of this either way, but the most important part is that you are intentionally using your TEA in the direction of transformation!

CHAPTER 8

Step 1, Part 1: Install Your MEL Values

*Step into and actualize the
Mindful Empowered Leader of
your inner world!*

–Glenn S. Cohen

The first part of step 1 is an exercise designed to focus you on your values and your present state of being. Values constitute what is most important to us in life, depending on the context in which we apply them. They govern our priorities and influence the choices we make day to day. Values act as our lighthouse, pointing us in the direction of our destiny and determining how we flow on our journey.

Your values are context-related and tend to center on what is most important to you regarding your relationships, family, health, wealth, work, adventure, purpose, spirituality, environment, politics, and more. Many times, your values were formed early in life by adapting to or adopting from how you made sense of your experiences with family, friends, and other influences.

Once you consciously or unconsciously chose what values were most important to you, you then developed beliefs associated with those values. A belief is the acceptance that a statement is true or that something exists. Next, you constructed rules for what had to happen or not happen for a belief to be true or false, which determined whether your values are being honored and fulfilled. These rules are part of your judgment system that leads you to assign green-empowered rules or red-disempowered rules.

We begin the next phase of the journey by associating with and activating empowered values to step into and actualize the MEL of our inner world. To gain the trust of our PODS, who have acted as our protective guardians for most of our lives, we need to associate with and actualize our MEL so that we are able to perform the neurological surgery to heal and free the younger versions of the self who are stuck, frozen in time within our inner world.

There are three sub-exercises in the MEL values exercise.

1. The first is a simple, easy, ninety-nine-day process that could have a profound impact on you and your life if you choose to follow the directions. While everything is optional, I absolutely encourage you to dedicate your TEA to this process.

2. The second is a fun exercise to leap into the future and describe yourself and your life in detail at some future time in which you are honoring and living as your MEL.

3. The third section is for those who wish to go the extra mile and get the most from your effort. Using meditative techniques, you can carve out new neural pathways to firmly encode the meanings behind the values and the intentions behind your beliefs.

Exercise 1:
Daily Ritual of Associating and Activating

Let's review the list of the MEL values. They are grouped into sets of four values, comprising nine groupings altogether.

Mindful Empowered Values

Being *present* and *nonjudgmental*
while remaining *centered* and *grounded*

Feeling *open* and *flexible*
with an abundance of *love* and *acceptance*

Showing *curiosity* and *inquisitiveness*
while offering *empathy* and *compassion*

Feeling *connected* and *vulnerable*
with a heart full of *gratitude* and *appreciation*

Having *patience* and *perseverance*
while embodying *confidence* and *courage*

Displaying *determination* and *discipline*
while *honoring* self and others with *integrity*

Focusing on *health* and *well-being*
while honoring your *purpose* and *spirituality*

Bringing *fun* and *laughter* into your life
while striving for *success* and *adventure*

Feeling *energized* and *inspired*
while continuously focusing on *growth* and *contribution*

Directions

- Mindfully associate with and activate each grouping of values. Take time in the morning to reflect on one grouping and remind yourself of it throughout the day. You will begin with the first grouping on the first day, the next day you'll move on to the second, and so on. When you complete the ninth and final grouping, you will start back again with the first grouping, until you have gone through each grouping eleven times, for ninety-nine days total.

- Decide on an anchor of awareness to remind you to focus on your exercise. Suggestions include anchoring to a piece of jewelry, such as a watch, bracelet, or ring—anything to remind you to apply the strategy throughout each day.

- Scan the QR code on page 310 to download and print several copies as reminders for yourself. Keep them somewhere prominent, such as a frame by your bed, on your refrigerator, or close to your desk.

- Mindfully manufacture massive amounts of sensory data to see, hear, feel, and sense the meaning of the values, so they become empowered directives to your unconscious mind. The more sensory data you use with AI and VAK It Up, the more effective you will be at installing these positive directives. This will increase your ability to reprogram yourself so that you can become unconsciously competent as your MEL.

Exploratory Questions

The following are some questions you can use to guide you through the day as you associate with and activate the meaning and intention of each value.

1. At the beginning of each day, reflect on the following questions for how you see, hear, feel, or sense each value showing up in your life when it comes to the pillars of your patterns—or your TEBS (thoughts, emotions, behaviors, and stories).

   - What does each value mean to me depending on the context?
   - What are my empowered thoughts regarding these values?
   - What positive emotions do I feel regarding these values?
   - What behaviors will I engage in to honor these values?

- What is my story—the narrative that wraps around the thoughts, emotions, and behaviors regarding these values?

2. As you go through your day, ask yourself the following questions:
   - How can I apply these empowered values into the present moment?
   - How can I apply these values for who I am being and what I am doing, depending on the context of the moment?
   - How can I relate these values to myself or whomever is in my focus of awareness at this time?

As an example, let's look at the first grouping: present, nonjudgmental, centered, grounded. As you go through the day, how might you apply the values so you show up honoring their meaning in the context you are presently engaged in? Think of how you would apply these values with respect to your relationship to yourself, partner, children, family, friends, colleagues, and clients.

Exercise 2:
Visit Your Future Self

Now, let's have some fun! This exercise is meant to help you see, hear, feel, and sense the amazing MEL you will grow into. Let's start with building a clear vision and story that will take you to your next highest level.

First, decide on a time in the future you would like to work with. Is it three months, six months, one year, five years, ten years from now, or something else? If you are focused on a goal, what is the date by which you would like to reach it? You can write down as many goals as you desire for different future timeframes.

Next, decide on how you will record your vision of your future self. Will you write in a journal, in a Word document, on the Notes app in your phone, or in the lines provided in this book?

Now, using all the MEL values, however they fit into your story about your future self, describe your vision and desires for your next highest version of yourself. Use the following list to guide you on where to focus your intention for this exercise. Pick at least one or two life realms from the list to build your new empowered future story.

Self	Relationships	Family	Career	Health & Fitness
Spirituality	Personal Growth	Finances	Social Life	Fun & Adventure

Use vivid detail, as if you were writing a fabulous script for your personal History Channel. Use lots of positive NSI keywords and phrases to depict this wonderful time in your life. Make sure your language is specific and realistically conveys the attainment of all your dreams, wishes, and desires for your future self.

Write this piece in the present tense and in a way that denotes that it is happening right now (because the unconscious mind will definitely pick up on this!). Use words that express the message that you are currently living this wonderful life in the present. Use your MEL values as guides for creating a story that evokes an embodied sense of empowerment.

As you write about the wonderful future life you're living as your green-empowered MEL, make sure you see what you see, hear what you hear, feel what you feel, and sense what you sense. Use as much positive sensory data as possible, through AI and VAK It Up (making sure your nonverbals match the VAK). Read aloud what you wrote, using the M3 strategy described on page 30 in the introduction (three times a day for thirty-three days), ensuring that you do so at a peak elevated energetic state, using a massive amount of sensory data to fire and wire in your amazing future self. Be sure to have fun with this and allow your future self to come alive!

_____

_____

_____

_____

_____

Exercise 3:
Die-Hard Programmers

You may want to go the extra mile to get the most you can from this exercise. I think you'll love it. You'll be spending time doing extra work to truly integrate and ingrain the MEL values into your references.

You will write a short story that brings in your values as they apply to a particular context or a challenge that you're currently facing. You can write multiple stories for various contexts of your life. For example, you may write about any challenges you are having with dis-empowered patterns in your inner world. You could also decide to focus on improving how you are showing up in your committed love relationship or in your professional life.

Directions

Write a paragraph for each set of values, depending on the context of your chosen challenge.

- What does each value mean to me?
  - Why is each value important to me? (E.g., "Being present helps me connect with my partner more meaningfully.")
  - What's the belief behind the meaning that makes this value important to me? (E.g., "Having a relationship with open communication makes my life calmer and happier.")

- Do I have any red-disempowered rules associated with the beliefs that need to be flipped to green? (E.g., "If my partner isn't present with me, that means they don't love me.")
- What does each value look like, sound like, and feel like in my life today? (Describe it as if you are already experiencing it right now, e.g., "My partner and I spend intentional time catching up on our day as we sit on our back porch, having a glass of wine together, watching the birds overhead, and drinking in the peace and beauty of the moment.")
- What would happen if I honored these values in the context of my life? (E.g., "I would feel more grounded, and my intimacy with my partner would improve exponentially.")
- What would happen if I did not honor these values in the context of my life? (E.g., "My relationship would probably end in the same way as my previous relationships, with both of us feeling unheard.")

_____

_____

_____

_____

_____

_____

- How do the values show up in my TEBS? (You can do this for each value, or for the ones that resonate the most for you, depending on your chosen context.)
  - What are my empowered thoughts regarding these values?
  - What positive emotions do I feel regarding these values?
  - What behaviors will I engage in to honor these values?
  - What is my story—the narrative that wraps around my thoughts, emotions, and behaviors with respect to these values?

_____

_____

_____

_____

_____

_____

- Use AI and VAK It Up to engage your TEBS with respect to your chosen value, in a short SIME.
  - Imagine that your chosen value is in your life today and watch it unfold, almost as if you were watching a movie in your mind's eye.
  - See it, hear it, feel it, sense it, and be it!
  - Use your breath to activate the meditation into a peak elevated state so that you can feel the positive emotion associated with the empowered meaning of the value you've chosen to work with, and remember to make sure your nonverbals match the VAK.
- Do this SIME each day for each set of values, until you go through each set eleven times for ninety-nine days, just as you did for the first exercise.
- Notice as you breathe in through your nose and out through your mouth in a natural, rhythmic manner. As you inhale deeply and exhale with intention, keep your body open, allowing energy to flow and listening for the messages from below.

Step 1, Part 2:
The Legend of Cenneuint:
An Interactive Read

Your unconscious mind will actualize
that which your conscious mind
chooses to believe.

—Glenn S. Cohen

This is the first experiential step of the Re-Claiming Process, which will guide you to go inside and explore your unlimited inner world. As you read the following fable (which you first came across at the end of volume 1), and as you ponder the questions included in the text, you will begin the process of discovering and understanding your NUBs, associating with and activating your MEL, and getting to know your PODS, offering them compassion without being submerged in them. The main character in this story is the Omni. The Omni is described as he/him in this story, but you can change that to she/her, whatever your preference is.

Use AI to see the story through your own eyes, as if you are embedded in the scene. Also use VAK It Up to make the story come to life—seeing, hearing, feeling, and sensing the journey as if you are the Omni, the protagonist of the story. Be mindful and curious as you notice what the story may bring up for you. Consider the following:

- How are you relating the story to your life?
- Does the story remind you of any challenges you may have faced in the past?
- Does the story remind you of any challenges you are dealing with in the present?
- What memories or images come up for you as you read the story?
- What emotions and feelings do you sense?
- What body sensations are you aware of?
- Are you aware of any patterns that seem eerily familiar to you in your own life?

Take time to reflect on each of the questions presented throughout the story to get the most out of this journey. Write the answers on the lines provided, in your journal, or on your digital device for future reference. And please remember to give yourself permission to listen for the messages to come up for you instead of thinking of the thoughts that come down to you. Give yourself permission to believe in the make-believe.

The questions included in the fable are designed to help guide you to go inside and explore your inner world. I suggest you read each question, then close your eyes and journey to whatever time and place the question leads your unconscious mind to go. If you find yourself thinking and searching for any answers, please stop yourself, and with loving kindness, take a deep breath, come back to the question, and allow your unconscious mind to present the answer to you. It may not come right away, and you may find that what comes up may very well be something that was not in your conscious awareness. This is wonderful news and a sign that you are letting the process work for you.

Please be patient and persevere as you make your way through the story and the questions; take as long as you need. Some questions may stretch you beyond your comfort zone, while others will place you in the scene the Omni is in so that you can see how the Omni's experience correlates to your own life. Most of all, have fun with this process and give yourself permission to let go of the present in order to explore your inner world—you'll be glad you did!

A while ago, in a place not far away, was a small village called Cenneuint. This community was tucked away in a valley surrounded by a large pasture of green grass and endless fields of sunflowers. On either side of the valley were majestic mountains with snow-covered peaks. At the base of the mountains to the east was a wide, flowing river filled with fish and fresh water supplied by the melting snow of the mountains.

The residents of Cenneuint ranged from newborns to elderly citizens. They lived in small, thatched huts that wound through the village in a circular maze. In the center of each hut was a trapdoor covered with an intricately woven rug. Under each trapdoor was a wooden shaft with steps leading down to a concealed basement used as a protective hiding place in case of danger.

There was a plaza in the center of the village where the people would gather to share, relate, and help one another. It was the hub of the village, a place of maximum belonging and connection. The Cenneuint people were led by the Omni and a council of advisers. Their role was to protect, support, and honor the values and resources of the village.

The Cenneuint people lived purposeful lives of happiness, fun, laughter, freedom, vulnerability, imperfection, and spontaneity. Their way of being was simple and flexible, and most of the time, they functioned in a peaceful, loving way.

However, things began to gradually change. Some of the younger ones were involved in or witnessed impactful neurological experiences with family members or others of significance. In these experiences, the young ones' sense of safety, certainty, and trust was threatened, violated, or ruptured—real or imagined. This caused their nervous systems to become activated at a high frequency, intensity, and duration.

As a young one, what experiences did you have that caused you to lose your sense of safety, certainty, and trust?

_____

_____

_____

Being so young, they did not have the awareness or skills to express, process, and integrate these stressful experiences. Unfortunately, they suffered neurological wounds, known as NUBs. Over time, the wounded ones felt challenged to cope with the uncomfortable body sensations arising from their painful emotions and disempowered beliefs. In response, they lost their sense of a secure attachment within and with others, and they started to change. They adopted new personae—roles they learned to play in order to hide and protect their vulnerable NUBs. This led them to disappear into the basement for periods of time. They began to think, feel, and act differently—either becoming rigid, quiet, and withdrawn or chaotic, loud, and aggressive.

As a young one, what experiences did you have that challenged you to cope with your painful emotions and disempowered beliefs?

_____

_____

_____

Describe any new roles or personae you created
and your reactive patterns for either getting
rigid and shutting down or chaotic and shouting out?

_____

_____

_____

Denial and despair fell upon the once happy, healthy, and harmonious village. Many of the caretakers went about their busy days ignoring the obvious, while others were worried about why this happened and how they could help the wounded youth.

How did your caregivers respond to your
verbal and nonverbal appeals for help?

_____

_____

_____

The members of the council of advisers were aware of a sacred ritual that could heal and free the suffering children from their inner bondage. They knew the Omni was the only person who could perform the healing process to assist the wounded ones to reveal, release, and resolve their dreaded NUBs. Unbeknownst to the villagers, the Omni felt tremendous pressure to do something to help. Over time, the Omni began to feel lost, dazed, and confused. He had never been challenged like this before. The Omni could not stop thinking about the neurological wounds infecting the youth and he began to succumb to a dark, scary, helpless feeling of being alone in his dilemma.

What younger versions of you exist
as NUBs in your nervous system today?

_____

_____

_____

When have you ever felt lost, dazed, and confused,
as if you'd fallen into a dark, scary place?

_____

_____

_____

The Omni knew, as the leader of Cenneuint, that he had the responsibility to heal and rescue the wounded youth. But he knew he had developed neither the knowledge nor skills to perform the sacred ritual of healing and freeing the children burdened by the dreaded NUBs. He was scared, unsure if he could follow in the footsteps of the ones who'd come before him.

One day, the Omni took a long walk and sat at the bank of the river to the east of the village. As he reflected on his challenge, he realized that he needed to reframe the story he was telling himself. The Omni wondered, *How can I change the meaning of what has happened so it serves me? What can I learn from this so it becomes a positive life lesson? What values can I resource so I become more resilient and can grow into the best Omni I can be?*

When you were confronted with a challenge,
how did you reframe the meaning?
What lessons did you learn?
Which values did you resource?

_____

_____

_____

He remembered hearing stories about previous Omnis who were faced with similar identity crises of being responsible for but not knowing how to help the infected youth with their vulnerable NUBs. The Omni remembered tales about how other leaders confronted with this challenge embarked on a journey of self-discovery. This led them into the vast unknown to uncover their inner truths, become enlightened, and learn the sacred ritual process. Once they did, they were able to return to Cenneuint to heal and rescue the wounded youth.

If you've ever hit rock bottom, what was that like?
How did you find your clarity?

_____

_____

_____

After a period of pondering, the Omni knew the only way he could fulfill his legacy was to go on his own journey. The Omni met with the council of advisers to inform them that he was leaving to embark on his journey to become empowered and find the secrets for how to perform the sacred ritual. That night, the Omni left the village, uncertain of where he was headed and when he would return.

How has your life journey
so far led you to this book?

_____

_____

_____

The council of advisers gathered the next day. They understood why the Omni had to leave, as they knew no one else could heal and rescue the wounded youth except him. They also knew that, now that the Omni was gone, the afflicted children needed protection. The members of the council met with the wounded youth and asked how they would like to be protected. The members then agreed to reassign themselves into various protective guardians. The newly anointed guardians worked together and swore an oath to do whatever they had to do to protect the vulnerable, suffering children. Some became defensive guardians. Proactive and vigilant, they excelled at scouting the environment to manage and control any perceived threats. They stayed at their post 24/7, without any sense of time, as they diligently performed their positive intention of protection.

In what ways have you constructed a protective pattern
to guard a vulnerable, unresolved NUB within you?

_____

_____

_____

Identify any proactive, defensive guardians
you have created who are vigilant about
managing and controlling your environment.

_____

_____

_____

Others volunteered to become offensive guardians due to their strength and specialized skill sets. They were strong, powerful, and never afraid to do whatever needed to be done. They stayed close to the boundary of the village in case anything slipped by the defensive guardians. They were reactive in nature and would quickly extinguish any threats, no matter how small or large, and had little to no concern for the consequences of their actions.

Identify any powerful, offensive guardians you created
that don't care about the consequences of their actions.

_____

_____

_____

Day in and day out, year after year, decade after decade, the guardians watched for any sign of danger. Many of the guardians worked together, while some grew resentful of one another, competing for the importance of their protective role.

For years, the Omni trekked up, over, and through the jagged mountains, venturing into thick forests with wild animals, swamps filled with fog and danger, and rivers with treacherous currents. Throughout the Omni's journey, he met many people from all backgrounds and walks of life. He asked for suggestions and advice to help him find the answers he was searching for. Over time, he began to realize the path he was on was not the rightful path he was *supposed* to be on. He slowly gained the awareness that he was not trusting his inner voice or developing the connection to his innate wisdom and intuition.

What challenges have you gone through on your journey of discovery up until this point in time?

_____

_____

_____

What happened that prompted you to notice that you were not listening to and honoring your inner voice?

_____

_____

_____

One day, as he sat marveling at a magnificent waterfall, the Omni had an epiphany. He realized he was allowing himself to be influenced by the cacophony of commentators from his past—the judgmental and critical voices talking over one another in his mind—as opposed to listening to the quiet whispers of wisdom coming up from his soul.

How do you get lost in the judgmental and critical stories that emerge from your mind's cacophony of commentators?

_____

_____

_____

On a beautiful sunny afternoon, the Omni came upon someone who was napping under a grand oak tree. As the Omni approached, the person awoke and asked the Omni to tell the story of what he was searching for. After listening and asking questions, the person said, "I am the Sage, an elder with wisdom and experience to share. I would like to offer you my service to act as your guide to help you find your answers."

The Omni thanked the Sage for their offer and asked for time to consider. The Omni took a while to listen for the messages coming up from his inner voice. After mindfully reflecting, he sensed a knowingness that this was the person to trust and allow to assist him on his adventure. As they journeyed into the unknown, the Sage shared their wisdom and insights with the Omni. Day after day, the Omni would listen, absorb, and begin to grasp and apply what the Sage was teaching.

What is your inner voice trying to share with you
at this time in your journey?

_____

_____

_____

A few weeks later, they came upon a crystal-clear lake in a valley nestled in the shadows of a mystical mountain range. The Sage suggested that the Omni walk over to the lake and look within. As the Omni stood there, he could see the reflection of an older, wiser version of himself in the water. This version of himself was compassionate and highly aware, and he seemed to have all the answers the Omni had been seeking. In that moment, the Omni could clearly hear the inner voice of this highest version of himself, providing clarity from deep within.

*Describe a time you stopped to listen to your inner voice
and made a choice that led you to find the
clarity and answers you were seeking.*

_____

_____

_____

As they ventured into the mountains beyond the lake, they came upon an opening on the side of the tallest mountain. The Omni sensed that the only way to the other side was to enter the opening. The Omni and the Sage camped outside for a time while the Sage continued to help the Omni work through his fears of the unknown. The Omni was still struggling with the thoughts and feelings haunting his mind of what he left behind. The Omni shared with the Sage, "Am I worthy to learn the sacred ritual? Am I good enough to actually heal and rescue the wounded ones? If I do return to Cenneuint, do I even belong there anymore? Will the villagers accept me as the Omni?"

*Identify any disempowered beliefs that
keep you stuck in the fear or shame of your story.*

_____

_____

_____

One evening, the Omni had a dream. In the dream, he came face-to-face with a large snake with a triangular head. The snake's voice sounded like the Sage's. It told the Omni that the only way to shed his skin of anger, sadness, fear, and shame was to go into the opening and find the mystic cave. It is there that the Omni would find his truth.

*As you explore your inner world, what choices could you make
to shed any protective layers that are holding you back?*

_____

_____

_____

When the Omni awoke, he shared the dream with the Sage, who smiled as the Omni pondered the meaning of the dream. It became a moment of clarity for the purpose of the Omni's journey. The Omni realized he needed to access his innate resources of patience and perseverance along with confidence and courage to go inside and challenge his inner fears. He realized that part of his journey was to become comfortable with that which is uncomfortable so he could have new experiences that would challenge him to grow into the highest version of himself. He recognized he needed to access and develop his innate resources.

*How can you tap into your innate resources of
patience and perseverance, with confidence and courage,
to work through the current challenges in your life?*

_____

_____

_____

Once inside, the Omni and the Sage kept walking through the twists and turns of endless tunnels until they came upon a cave deep within the mountain. As they entered the cave, the Omni knew this was where he was meant to be.

The Omni and the Sage wandered for days, and the Omni spoke of an uncomfortable feeling arising from the uncertainty of being in the cave. The Omni sensed the cave was sending him a message, guiding him to go deeper inside to seek the answers he was searching for. All the while, the Sage patiently shared wisdom and knowledge, preparing the Omni for the eventuality the Sage foresaw. For, as far off as it seemed to the Omni, the Sage had no doubt that the Omni would come to face his greatest fear and do the inner work that was necessary to go home and rescue the wounded ones.

What would it look, sound, and feel like
to deal with your uncomfortable feelings of uncertainty
until the feelings subside and clarity appears?

_____

_____

_____

One day, the Omni came upon a door hidden in the walls of the cave. Sensing he must open the door to find his answers, the Omni pushed against the door and stood there, shocked at the sight before him. In the darkness, the Omni could see multiple glowing pairs of eyes looking back at him. He knew the eyes he saw were the eyes of the wounded ones pleading for the Omni to return to Cenneuint to heal and rescue them.

Imagine you are looking within.
How many pairs of eyes (belonging to your NUBs)
do you sense are crying out for you to rescue them?

_____

_____

_____

In that moment, the Omni heard the voice of the Sage say, "Congratulations. Omni, you have completed your hero's journey and discovered your bliss. You have earned the title of Mindful Empowered Leader of Cenneuint. You will now finish imprinting all the mindful empowered values and learn the strategies, tools, and techniques to perform the sacred ritual over the next eighty-eight days. You will then leave the cave, go back to Cenneuint, and take your rightful place as the Mindful Empowered Leader. You will earn the trust of the guardians and then heal and rescue the wounded youth."

The Omni expressed gratitude and appreciation to the Sage, for it was the Sage who had guided him to actualize his purpose by associating with and activating his mindful empowered values and learning the sacred ritual. After the eighty-eighth day, the Omni left the cave with his strategies, tools, techniques, and values firmly ingrained.

What would it look, sound, and feel like to step into the MEL of your inner world and discover your unique bliss?

_____

_____

_____

With tremendous pride, passion, and purpose, the Mindful Empowered Omni made his way through all forms of terrain until he stood at the top of the mountain overlooking the village from where he'd begun his journey so many years ago. As the Omni approached the outer boundary of the village, he knew the guardians had no idea who he was, since he had been gone for many moons. The guardians had been protecting the village day in and day out, not knowing any semblance of time or space.

As you stand on the top of your mountain and gaze ahead to the future, what does it look, sound, and feel like from the perspective of your MEL?

_____

_____

_____

As the Omni approached, he knew he had two options. He could either get reactive by denying, defending, deflecting, debating, and dismissing why he had left, what had happened to him, and why he was there now. Or he could choose to be responsive and show up mindfully by being available and attuning and aligning with, acknowledging, and assuring the guardians by honoring and respecting their positive protective purpose for guarding the youth.

When you are triggered and faced with a challenge,
which way do you choose to go?

_____

_____

_____

The Omni knew he would be met with resistance, so he chose to be a responsive receiver of their messages. As he approached and introduced himself, the guardians shouted, "We have no idea who you are! We have been guarding the wounded ones forever. You show up out of nowhere and expect us to trust you? If you are the Mindful Empowered Leader of Cenneuint, then you abandoned and neglected us and your wounded youth."

Describe the last time you heard your inner commentators
argue with you because they didn't trust you.

_____

_____

_____

The Omni knew he had to do whatever he could to create safety, certainty, and trust with each of the guardians. He said, "I hear your concerns and completely understand. There is a round campsite with a firepit 333 feet from the gates of the village. Why don't we all go over there to sit and talk?"

Using AI and VAK It Up, visualize the number of guardians you see, sitting on the benches in front of you now.

_____

_____

_____

The guardians accepted the Omni's invitation, and they all walked over to the ceremonial firepit where the guardians took a seat on benches encircling the fire. The Omni sat in a special chair carved from ancient wood with the letters *MEL* etched into the top. The Omni remembered the lessons the Sage had shared and knew he needed to establish a secure attachment bond with each of the guardians, honoring his mindful empowered values of:

- showing up *present, nonjudgmental, centered,* and *grounded* as he listened to each of the guardians' stories;
- transmitting *openness, flexibility, love,* and *acceptance* toward the guardians;
- displaying *curiosity, inquisitiveness, empathy,* and *compassion* for the guardians and what they had endured;

- feeling *connected, vulnerable, grateful,* and *appreciative* for how long and hard the guardians had worked to protect the wounded ones; and
- having *patience, perseverance, confidence,* and *courage* to gain the guardians' trust.

Which of the MEL values do you need to activate the most when you face a challenge or meet your PODS?

_____

_____

_____

One by one, each of the guardians told their story about how they had volunteered to reassign themselves and develop well-intended strategies to protect the wounded youth. The Omni listened and reflected on what he heard from each of the guardians in such a way that allowed each guardian to feel seen, heard, understood, validated, and empathized with.

Pick one guardian and listen to its story.
What is the strategy of protection for this particular PODS?
Close your eyes and really listen to the messages
that are coming up for you.

_____

_____

_____

The Omni knew that to get permission to enter the village and free the wounded youth, he would need all the guardians to answer the primary attachment question—*Are you there for me, the way I need you, when I need you the most?*—with an enthusiastic yes. The Omni knew he had ruptured that bond and had not been there for the guardians and the infected children, the way they'd needed him, when they'd needed him the most.

What positive, innate aspect of self
did you reassign into a protective personality
because you sensed someone was not there for you,
the way you needed them, when you needed them the most?

_____

_____

_____

As the Omni began to create a secure attachment to each of the guardians, they began to share their greatest fears about what would happen if they did not fulfill their positive protective purpose. They told the Omni their job was to do whatever they could so the wounded ones would not get triggered and activate the original painful emotions and disempowered beliefs residing within their vulnerable NUBs— which could have disastrous consequences.

Listen to the story of the PODS you picked.
What is its greatest fear, and what unresolved
painful emotion and disempowered belief is it protecting?

_____

_____

_____

The Omni expressed respect for how the members of the council had volunteered to reassign into protective guardians, giving up their original innate qualities. He conveyed his utmost gratitude and appreciation to each for how tired they must be and how long and hard they had worked to protect the wounded ones.

Acknowledging how long and hard it has worked for you,
go ahead and express your respect, gratitude, and
appreciation for your PODS.

The Omni asked each of the guardians, one by one, if they trusted him to be the Mindful Empowered Leader, and if not, he totally understood. The Omni explained that they would continue their discussion, and he would do whatever they needed until he fully gained the guardians' full trust.

At this moment, does your PODS trust you
as the Mindful Empowered Leader of your inner world?
Don't worry if the answer is no;
you will do the work to gain their trust
as you proceed on your journey.

When all the guardians agreed to trust the Omni, he asked each guardian for permission to enter the village. The Omni explained that he would need their permission to perform the sacred ritual to heal and free the wounded ones. Once the guardians granted him permission to go into the village, they shared where the infected youth were hiding.

Did your PODS give you
unconditional permission to go to your wounded ones?

_____

_____

_____

The Omni and the guardians then walked through the gates of the village and stood in front of each hut where there was a suffering child hiding. The Omni asked each of the afflicted children if they would give him permission to talk with them. When they said yes, the Omni journeyed to meet them, wherever they were, stuck, frozen in time. All the while, the guardians watched diligently, making sure the wounded ones' NUBs did not become triggered. The Omni then apologized for abandoning and neglecting them for so long and asked forgiveness for not hearing their cries for help earlier. Once the little ones expressed forgiveness, the Omni witnessed each of their stories to begin the process of establishing a secure attachment bond. The Omni listened and reassured each of them that he was the Mindful Empowered Leader and asked if they would trust him.

How old is your wounded one,
and where are they stuck, frozen in time?
Note that you may encounter more than one wounded one.

_____

_____

_____

Does your wounded one
forgive and trust you?

_____

_____

_____

Once the bond of safety, certainty, and trust was repaired, the wounded youth shared their stories of how they had developed their vulnerable NUBs, containing the painful emotions and disempowered beliefs of an impactful neurological experience they'd had during a certain time.

What's the story of your impactful neurological experience?
What painful emotions and disempowered beliefs are stuck
within your NUB?

_____

_____

_____

The Omni then led each through the arduous sacred ritual to reveal, release, and resolve the vulnerable NUBs so the infected ones could express, process, and integrate back into their original innate wholeness. Once each was healed of their burdens from the past, they glowed with peace and vibrated with joy as they integrated their new green-empowered sense of being. They were now able to fully access their positive, innate aspects of being vulnerable, loving, valuable, joyful, playful, spontaneous, and free.

What would it be like to see, hear, and feel
your wounded one as free to be its original, innate, whole self?

_____

_____

_____

The Omni and the guardians returned to the campsite and sat down and the Omni asked each of the guardians: "Now that the younger ones are healed and free and you do not need to protect them anymore, what would you like to do now?"

The Omni explained that they could either go back to their original role, the way they were before they were reassigned, or they could adopt a new, empowered, alternative pattern and rejoin the family in that role. One by one, each of the guardians transformed into their desired empowered pattern and then they all went into the village.

Ask your PODS what innate values or
empowered resources they would love to transform into.

_____

_____

_____

That evening, they had a huge celebration and danced all night. The villagers had all finally regained their sense of safety, certainty, and trust. Their hopes and dreams of the Omni returning to fulfill his legacy to heal and rescue the wounded ones had been actualized!

They restored their sense of inner peace with an overwhelming feeling of joy and gratitude as they reclaimed their original innate wholeness. Their inner family was happily reintegrated back into a flexible, peaceful system, with the Omni taking his rightful place as the Mindful Empowered Leader of Cenneuint.

What would it look, sound, and feel like
to heal your NUBs, free yourself from the past,
and celebrate achieving your next highest version of self?

_____

_____

_____

CHAPTER 10

Step 1, Part 3: Meet and Greet Your PODS

Listen for the messages to come up for you
instead of thinking of the thoughts
that come down to you!

–Glenn S. Cohen

Now, we come to the part of the Re-Claiming Process that is designed to help you understand and get to know your PODS. If you've read volume 1, you'll recognize that this is a repetition of the material you learned in chapter 7 in that volume. It's a good idea to continue to revisit this part of the process over time; as we start to untangle from the voices of our internal cacophony of commentators, it's likely that new or buried PODS will rise to the surface to get your attention. Even if you went through the exercise in volume 1, I encourage you to do it again here. The process of learning, stretching, healing, and growing requires us to revisit our PODS periodically and see if the dynamics we've experienced have changed.

Remember, you formed these aspects of self at some point in your life to protect unresolved vulnerable aspects of yourself, known as NUBs, which are bundles of neurons containing energy and information that have metaphorically fractured off from your nervous system and become stuck, frozen in time, in your body. PODS usually originate in childhood and can also be reinforced or formed in your adult life. This occurs when an INE is not expressed, processed, and integrated back into the nervous system, which creates neurological wounding.

PODS are adaptive personalities that live in your nervous system; they are usually experienced as a body sensation between the throat and groin. PODS have been reassigned from an innate role into a protective role. They have their own TEBS. They usually do not act alone and are part of your intricate inner world. Their primary positive purpose is to guard your inner children and wounded adults from getting triggered and being overwhelmed by the original painful emotions they felt. PODS will reenact old patterns to reinforce their protective roles, thereby creating cycles to validate your own TEBS.

PODS come in two forms: defensive and offensive.

- *Defensive PODS* are proactive, covert, vigilant, and on the lookout for danger—real or imagined. PODS are usually on duty to manage and control their environment. They focus on distracting and deflecting from feeling painful emotions, and they activate disempowered beliefs in a mistaken belief that this will protect the NUBs.
- *Offensive PODS* are reactive, overt, and at their extreme will destroy a relationship, a career, or your body without concern for the consequences. These PODS activate when your nervous system has been triggered above an NSI of 6. They focus on blocking and inhibiting the painful emotions and disempowered beliefs from being activated.

Preparation for the Process

There are three sections to this exercise:
- Identifying and rating all the PODS you relate to.

- Identifying the top five PODS that influence your life today.
- Identifying your top five PODS' weapons of choice.

This exercise is designed for you to become acquainted with your PODS, whom you can see as your multiple protective personalities. This is a process that connects your conscious mind with your unconscious mind so you can begin integrating your inner and outer worlds.

Remember to utilize AI, VAK It Up, and your BSI to create a more vivid experience of encountering your PODS, just as you did in the previous chapter.

Section 1:
Identify Your PODS

It's time to meet your PODS! PODS stem from unresolved neurological wounding. PODS have a positive purpose to guard the NUBs they protect and do not realize that their strategies no longer serve the present-day version of you. Again, if you read volume 1, you completed this exercise. I advise you to re-score your PODS from your new perspective after you have completed the work you have been doing up to now.

I have arranged the following list of PODS in order from defensive to offensive, but it is by no means exhaustive. These PODS are common ones I've identified from years of working with clients. Below each PODS, I have listed some of its common characteristics and strategies. These are examples and suggestions for you to review to see if you identify with any of the descriptors. *You may identify with some, none, or all.* You may notice that some PODS are similar. You can choose to combine them or come up with new ones on your own.

These characteristics and strategies are not your conscious, everyday MEL patterns, but reactive patterns that get activated when you perceive danger and become triggered. Remember that PODS come out to play when they perceive some form of danger, real or imagined. Defensive PODS are more proactive and covert and may be activated more often at low levels of reactivity, as we try to manage and control our environment, while offensive PODS are activated at higher levels of reactivity, when the threat level is greater. The PODS may only be infrequently present but can unduly influence your inner and outer world. So, please be honest, authentic, vulnerable, open, and real with yourself. Score this exercise not on an understanding of who you *think* you are but from the perspective of how you actually show up when you are triggered.

As you work through the exercise, note the words, phrases, and sentences that resonate with you. Perhaps there are images of specific people or archetypes that come to the surface as you encounter each of these PODS. Maybe you can feel the body sensation that is associated with being in the thrall of these aspects of self. Let yourself be playful and nonjudgmental, and feel free to involve your visual, auditory, and kinesthetic (body) awareness.

As you read through the list, place a check mark to the left of each of the characteristics that are familiar to you; you may wish to underline any keywords and phrases that resonate. Then, for each of the PODS, give yourself a ranking from 0 to 10. Zero means you never display any of the pattern, and 10 represents the highest frequency or intensity of that pattern in how it shows up in your life. I have provided a few lines after each PODS for you to write about how it resonates with you. Describe any thoughts or awareness that come up for you and how this PODS shows up in your life, as well as the language of its story and the consequences this has on your inner and outer world when the PODS is active. Also list any characteristics that are not listed and that you feel exemplify this PODS for you.

_____ **Codependent**—Has difficulty forming a healthy, mutually satisfying relationship. They are addicted to relationships but often form ones that are one-sided, abusive, or destructive of self or other.

- [ ] Too little self-esteem and inability to nourish a healthy self-love
- [ ] Too much self-esteem and the belief that they deserve excessive self-love

- [ ] Diminishes others' self-esteem
- [ ] Is boundaryless and allows others to walk all over them
- [ ] Uses boundaries to wall off from others
- [ ] Habitually busts other people's boundaries
- [ ] Doesn't listen to their inner voice, allowing other people to manipulate them
- [ ] Excessively believes in their knowingness, thinking they know all
- [ ] Plays the gaslighting game to mess with other people's minds
- [ ] Is utterly without wants and needs, and doesn't ask anything of others
- [ ] Needs and wants excessively, which makes them act clingy and desperate
- [ ] Withholds from fulfilling others' needs and wants
- [ ] Believes they have no control over their inner and outer world
- [ ] Overly controls their inner and outer world
- [ ] Manipulates others' inner and outer worlds

_____

_____

_____

_____ **Pleaser-Appeaser**—Is usually overly empathetic, thoughtful, and caring, which may originate from a low level of self-esteem.

- [ ] Acts like the maid and takes responsibility for everything and everyone
- [ ] Is submissive, over-apologetic, or overcompensating in relationships, allowing others to take advantage of them or boss them around
- [ ] Gets annoyed after giving so much of the self and sometimes sacrificing their own needs and wants
- [ ] Resents others for not reciprocating
- [ ] Controls their environment and focuses on overachievement

☐ Mirrors others' reactions and behaviors while trying to avoid making waves

_____ **Martyr**—May overly sacrifice their own needs and wants in order to "do for" others.

☐ Acts like a flight attendant, serving everyone else's needs without question

☐ Pretends to do for others with joy at the time, yet usually their actions come from a sense of obligation or guilt

☐ Feels emotions of resentment, contempt, or anger and a perception of powerlessness

☐ Has a pattern of being a caretaker and makes unnecessary sacrifices

☐ Falls on their own sword under the guise of virtue

☐ Overly generous, cajoling, or self-righteous with a savior complex

_____ **Scapegoat**—Takes on projected guilt or shame and may serve as an emotional punching bag for others' projected negative emotions.

☐ Puts self down, helping others to feel superior and enabling themselves to not deal with their own weaknesses

☐ Punishes self for the same mistake or series of perceived failures, even when others have long since excused or forgiven them

☐ May feel guilty, rueful, ashamed, or embarrassed

- [ ] When scapegoating others, feels a sense of superiority and pride
- [ ] May have feelings of entitlement and grandiosity, with limited personal self-reflection
- [ ] May display poor character, self-righteousness, or hypocrisy

_____

_____

_____

_____ **Broom Sweeper**—Needs to sweep what they feel is unsightly out of sight.

- [ ] Acts like an ostrich burying its head in the sand
- [ ] Denies reality and will not accept responsibility
- [ ] Is good at blaming and accusing others in order to deflect from the truth
- [ ] Protects the dirt under the rug and becomes activated by any threat of exposure
- [ ] Loves to keep secrets, usually associated with a sense of fear, shame, or guilt
- [ ] If the dirt pile gets exposed, may initiate an offensive PODS to protect whatever it is hiding

_____

_____

_____

_____ **Critic/Analytic**—May blame themselves for negative situations and seldom gives themselves compliments.

- [ ] The voice of this PODS may resemble a parental voice speaking down to you
- [ ] Gets down on self as a person, as opposed to specific mistakes they make, and persists in overanalyzing mistakes
- [ ] Doesn't easily forgive

☐ Is usually never satisfied with achievements and has very high standards, often punishing self or others for not meeting their unrealistic standards

☐ Has a pattern of worry and "what if" scenarios with black-and-white thinking

☐ Usually never asks for help and does not assert their own needs and desires

☐ Often compares self to someone else and typically comes up short

☐ Has trouble accepting compliments and may become defensive in the face of feedback

☐ Acts judgmental, argumentative, or hypervigilant

_____

_____

_____

_____ **Procrastinator**—Will put off doing what they know needs to be done in order to validate a disempowered belief.

☐ Usually very good at justifying and excusing their procrastinating choices

☐ Has beliefs that are associated with not enough, not belonging, or not being accepted

☐ Tends to become defensive when called out on procrastinating

☐ Often feels overwhelmed and is easily distracted

☐ Tends to be disorganized and lose track of time

☐ Operates on fear and has challenges maintaining a clear vision

☐ Spins in mental circles

_____

_____

_____

_____ **Perfectionist**—Is usually a high achiever with an all-or-nothing thinking pattern.

- [ ] May have rigid patterns and unreasonable standards for themselves and others
- [ ] Sets high goals, works hard, and strives to be the best at anything they do
- [ ] Tends to be a rule follower and may be highly critical, driven by fear of failure or loss
- [ ] May have unrealistic expectations for their own abilities or stamina and takes criticism personally
- [ ] Is envious of others
- [ ] Focuses on meeting others' expectations for performance to the detriment of their own neurological, mental, emotional, physical, or spiritual health
- [ ] Appears obsessive, insecure, high-strung, anxious, hypervigilant, or self-critical

_____

_____

_____

_____ **Competitor**—Is seen as a Type A personality.

- [ ] Operates at a fast pace, demonstrating high levels of impatience and a dislike for wasting time
- [ ] Displays rigid patterns and gets easily triggered, associating self-worth with achievement
- [ ] May have a high comfort level with conflict and competition and can be aggressive in their offers and concessions
- [ ] Is independent versus interdependent; loves a challenge but doesn't like to be challenged
- [ ] Enjoys debating substantive issues but is not a great listener
- [ ] Uses combative ways of communicating
- [ ] May be labeled as conceited, self-absorbed, too picky, full of themselves, inflexible, or passive-aggressive

☐ Spends a lot of time focused on work and their goals

☐ Has difficulty receiving feedback; takes failure personally; has been known to lie, deceive, manipulate, or steal to win

_____

_____

_____

_____ **Superhero**—Believes they are invincible and that they have superhuman strength.

☐ Tries to save the world to avoid themselves

☐ Pretends they have endless energy and must always be doing something

☐ May display a pattern of acting like they wear a Teflon suit— nothing gets in or out emotionally

☐ Wants to be the best and will work tirelessly to prove it

☐ Believes they can fight through life's challenges with no break or need for rest

☐ Perceives there are unmet needs to achieve and always tries to accomplish more

☐ May have an unhealthy sense of responsibility

☐ Wants to help and meet everyone's needs and often takes on a workload that is meant to be shared

☐ Feels useless if they can't help someone

☐ Often does not know how to say no or accept the disappointment or criticism of anyone around them

_____

_____

_____

_____ **Chameleon**—Is also known as the Great Pretender.

☐ Can win an Oscar for best actress or actor

MEET AND GREET YOUR PODS

- [ ] Adapts into whatever they need to be while keeping their private self hidden
- [ ] Blends seamlessly into any social environment
- [ ] Walks into a room and quickly picks up on the expectations of those around them
- [ ] Becomes the life of the party or a quiet, thoughtful participant
- [ ] Changes and plays any role to gain connection and significance
- [ ] Pays close attention to social cues and may mimic the behavior of others
- [ ] Displays flexibility and can be very skillful in reinventing themselves as a particular situation dictates
- [ ] May be skilled at lying and a master of soothing rocking boats when social situations go awry

_____

_____

_____

_____ **Comedian**—Uses humor to deflect uncomfortable feelings.
- [ ] Uses humor to relieve discomfort by projecting any anxious or fearful feelings outward
- [ ] Deploys passive-aggressive verbal and nonverbal darts to feel better than others
- [ ] Usually has low self-esteem and is somewhat truthful in their self-deprecation
- [ ] Can be skillful at sweeping important matters under the rug with a joke or barbed comment
- [ ] May use self-insults or jokes from an armory of prepared comebacks
- [ ] Usually likes to deflect responsibility
- [ ] May tell jokes at inappropriate times and laugh in somber moments
- [ ] Acts insufferably, can be cringeworthy, and depends on wit over substance

☐ May use animated nonverbals to display their comical messages

_____

_____

_____

_____ **Worrywart**—Perceives their environment with caution and wariness.

☐ May have high anxiety and be sensitive to uncertainty
☐ The thought of something frightening can induce body sensations, such as panic attacks or a freeze state
☐ Fearful if they perceive they are not following preset rules
☐ Can be anxious, hypervigilant, intrusive, or distrustful
☐ May obsess over problems without attempting to resolve them
☐ Views the glass as being half-empty and may unconsciously create problems when they sense things are going too well by reenacting and reinforcing disempowered patterns to validate their role

_____

_____

_____

_____ **Pit of Sorrow**—Carries the burden of sadness from the past and projects it onto the present.

☐ Walks around with a perpetual gray cloud over their head
☐ Looks to others to validate their story of grief, pain, and sadness to gain connection and significance
☐ May feel devastated, anguished, or overwhelmed by sadness, grief, or shame
☐ Sees through a lens of pessimism and may feel physical pain that stems from sorrowful emotions
☐ May have given up on trying to feel better and cannot see a way out of their story of sorrow

_____ _____ _____

_____ _____ _____

_____ _____ _____

_____ **Grinch**—Has a pattern of being an unpleasant grouch and may display a wicked temper.

- ☐ Is a taker not a giver, and dismisses attempts to connect or be vulnerable
- ☐ Has challenges feeling and sensing empathy and compassion for self and others
- ☐ Has a sour attitude with a depressed judgment
- ☐ Seems greedy, grumpy, or gluttonous
- ☐ Is usually sad and distrustful and seems to be out to ruin everyone else's joy
- ☐ Uses their acquisitions to build walls between themselves and others
- ☐ Acts like the greatest but only chases what society tells them to chase
- ☐ May be status seeking, vain, bratty, dismissive, or holier-than-thou

_____ _____ _____

_____ _____ _____

_____ _____ _____

_____ **Hermit Crab**—Builds walls or suits of armor to protect the self from perceived threats.

- ☐ Tends to withdraw, shut down, or hide until the coast is clear—is a great escape artist
- ☐ Usually engages in stonewalling and not being vulnerable and blocks connection to others to protect self
- ☐ Will retreat into their shell and become rigid if they perceive chaos

- [ ] Will act impenetrable and emotionless when they feel afraid, distrustful, reserved, or skeptical
- [ ] May disassociate and act as if they are immune to the severity of a situation
- [ ] May be unable to engage others until the intensity of a situation subsides

_____

_____

_____

_____ **Hall Passer**—Finds ingenious ways of giving themselves an out and does not hold themselves accountable.

- [ ] Similar to the Procrastinator, is good at avoiding self-accountability
- [ ] Will make up an elaborate story to prove themselves right, in order to get away with acting out in some way
- [ ] Debates, deflects, and defends their disempowered story to enable and embolden the thoughts and behaviors of the pattern
- [ ] Usually acts from low self-esteem and enhanced fear of failure
- [ ] Sweeps negative emotions and behaviors under the rug
- [ ] May act as the fun one who says, "The hell with it—let's go have a good time!"

_____

_____

_____

_____ **Space Cadet**—Is sometimes associated with a Type B personality.

- [ ] Attempts to lower others' perceptions of their intelligence and capabilities
- [ ] Lives within their own rainbow-sparkly-unicorn inner world

- [ ] Is often impatient with a relatively short attention span and lack of attention to detail
- [ ] Uses this pattern to disengage with reality
- [ ] May seem oblivious, dazed, or unaware
- [ ] May be driven by fear of the unknown or avoid vulnerability and responsibility
- [ ] Masterfully deflects and can be excellent at pretending to be spaced-out in order to avoid dealing with reality

_____

_____

_____

_____ **Left-Brainer**—Is also known as the Solver.
- [ ] May be a rigid thinker, relying heavily on patterns associated with the left brain: linear, logical, linguistic, list maker, and orderly
- [ ] Usually tries to fix or solve a problem or create a problem to fix
- [ ] Seems aloof and calculated and approaches situations as black or white, right or wrong
- [ ] May act like a professor and lecture others, thinking they know it all due to their brilliant left brain
- [ ] May act like a supreme court judge or enjoy playing chess with other people's minds
- [ ] May have challenges with discussions and sharing their feelings and inner world
- [ ] May have difficulty in committed love relationships and connecting with their heart instead of their head

_____

_____

_____

_____ **Rebel**—Can be bitter and cynical, and they are often unhappy and can act like a headstrong child.

- ☐ Wants to go against the grain and break established rules
- ☐ Can have their rebellious patterns intensified by other people's attempts at reasoning or logic
- ☐ May find the thought of accepting authority triggering and has a strong preference for doing things their way
- ☐ Possibly stoic or a loner, ambivalent, defiant, and could be considered a "bad influence"
- ☐ May disregard the reasons for rules even though the outcomes are likely to be painful or pose a disadvantage to them
- ☐ Tries to assert a sense of power and control over others in order to compensate for real or imagined inner weakness

_____

_____

_____

_____ **Tester**—Is usually manipulative, defiant, and associated with patterns of distrust.

- ☐ Crosses boundaries in obvious and subtle ways and uses passive-aggressive tactics to gauge if their needs are being met
- ☐ Is compelled to unconsciously test others to falsely gain a sense of safety, certainty, and trust
- ☐ Seeks to gain significance and connection with dysfunctional strategies
- ☐ Will test others, especially a committed love partner, to prove that a disempowered belief is true
- ☐ Usually, the person whom they are testing must pass five tests in a row in order for the PODS to regain a sense of safety, certainty, and trust

_____

_____

_____

_____ **Seducer**—Uses their attractiveness to allure others, which gives them a way of empowering themselves.

- ☐ Uses their good looks and charm to seduce or taunt others
- ☐ Uses seduction to manipulate others to satisfy their own needs and wants
- ☐ Is skilled at being cunning and misleading
- ☐ Uses nonverbals to arouse others' passions and hopes, then leaves quickly when they get what they want
- ☐ Seeks to gain connection and significance from their attractiveness and sex appeal
- ☐ Generally avoids true vulnerability and commitment

_____

_____

_____

_____ **Zinger**—Loves to throw passive-aggressive darts and highlight others' shortcomings.

- ☐ Uses verbal and nonverbal methods to gain interest or to surprise and shock
- ☐ Usually reacts to someone or something that is perceived as threatening their vulnerability
- ☐ Comes across as a smartass or sassy-pants
- ☐ Uses sarcastic humor to project uncomfortable inner emotions
- ☐ May act like a spoiled brat if they do not get their way
- ☐ Uses pointed, witty language
- ☐ Loves to play the "gotcha" game and enjoys seeing others squirm

_____

_____

_____

_____ **Chief Executive**—May try to cope by controlling others.

- ☐ Has a compulsive need to manage their environment to feel comfortable
- ☐ Wants to control the outcome when they sense uncertainty
- ☐ Displaces their sense of discomfort by barking orders and directions
- ☐ May be rigid with their rules
- ☐ Will become reactive if they sense any form of danger
- ☐ May call forth the Control Freak to take over if they fail in their duties

_____

_____

_____

_____ **Bouncer**—Misguided in their inflated ego or physical presence.

- ☐ Blocks self from vulnerability and others from connecting with them
- ☐ Acts powerfully to enforce rules and strives for alignment with authority figures
- ☐ May display a superior posture to intimidate others in order to feel better about themselves
- ☐ Is often hypervigilant and insecure
- ☐ May get defensive when others try to connect
- ☐ Can stonewall or push others away to avoid the realization that their perception does not match up to reality

_____

_____

_____

_____ **Manipulator**—Uses their brain power to mess with others' minds. They are also known as the Salesperson or the Gaslighter.

- ☐ Targets others, knowing others' weaknesses well
- ☐ Makes up stories, lies, and deceives in order to create confusion
- ☐ Might play the victim and use passive-aggressive nonverbals without regard for healthy boundaries
- ☐ Likes to pressure others and not give much time for others to make decisions
- ☐ Avoids responsibilities and justifies, excuses, and rationalizes their choices

_____

_____

_____

_____ **Defense Attorney**—Can be a defensive or offensive PODS.

- ☐ Works to shield themselves from accountability or punishment
- ☐ Questions incessantly to prove their point and present a case to defend their TEBS
- ☐ Is prone to defend, debate, deny, and deflect
- ☐ Is dismissive of others' thoughts and emotions
- ☐ Makes others feel like they are being interrogated on the witness stand
- ☐ Makes plea bargains to manage their vulnerable emotions

_____

_____

_____

_____ **Prosecuting Attorney**—Can be a defensive or offensive PODS.
- [ ] Gets in others' faces and argues their case
- [ ] Can be aggressive and quick to judge or condemn
- [ ] Fears criticism and will challenge other people's thoughts and beliefs to prove them wrong
- [ ] To prove their case, may be vicious with their nonverbals to provoke others
- [ ] Points fingers, pursues, and pushes buttons to get a reaction
- [ ] Picks apart language to ensure the other person is guilty
- [ ] Will attack others' perspective in order to make their case and prove a disempowered story to be right—at all costs

_____

_____

_____

_____ **Control Freak**—May be compulsive with decisions and obsessed with work, cleaning, and organizing.
- [ ] Is overly concerned with others' opinions
- [ ] Tends to criticize self and others
- [ ] Does not acknowledge when someone does something right—everything must be perfect, even themselves
- [ ] May become irrationally angry if someone doesn't answer a text right away
- [ ] Makes mean comments about someone in front of others
- [ ] Has difficulty being vulnerable or feeling intense emotions
- [ ] Can be passive-aggressive, obsessive, mood-dysregulated, over-anxious, depressed, or phobic
- [ ] Constantly reorganizes and reformats reality
- [ ] May be demanding when others rock the boat
- [ ] Sweeps under the rug what they think is unsightly, unbecoming, or incriminating, but eventually runs out of space to hide all the dirt

_____

_____

_____

_____ **Catastrophizer**—Assumes that the worst will happen.

- ☐ May adopt the pattern of a helpless victim
- ☐ Often believes that they are in a worse situation than they really are or exaggerates the difficulties they face
- ☐ May be hypervigilant, pessimistic, self-sabotaging, or self-limiting
- ☐ Makes themselves the focus of entire conversations, events, or situations
- ☐ Uses catastrophic or hyperbolic disempowered language to tell their story
- ☐ Makes twos into eights or mountains out of molehills, using words and phrases like _the sky is falling_ and _the other shoe is about to drop_

_____

_____

_____

_____ **Fortress**—The Fort Knox of all PODS is the offensive cousin of the Hermit Crab.

- ☐ Will stonewall, shut down, freeze up, or disappear when they sense threats
- ☐ Can be totally emotionless and unable to communicate or connect
- ☐ Disassociates from the present and acts unaware about the severity of a situation
- ☐ May be unable to engage others until hours, days, or weeks after a challenging situation occurs

_____

_____

_____

_____ **JERC-Off**—(The *justifications*, *excuses*, *rationalizations*, and *cajoling*, if you want the full name!) is the offensive cousin to the Hall Passer PODS.

- ☐ When the Hall Passer's hall pass is no longer effective, the JERC-Off might take over
- ☐ Says and does anything to justify their story
- ☐ Makes up excessive excuses to protect their intention
- ☐ Rationalizes their decisions and actions to defend their story
- ☐ Loves to cajole and mess with others' reality to defend and protect themselves

_____

_____

_____

_____ **Hurricane**—Is the offensive cousin to the Rebel PODS.

- ☐ If the Rebel is unable to accomplish their goals, they may call upon the Hurricane to destroy that which they could not control
- ☐ Will go off and create absolute mayhem, no matter where they are or whom they are with
- ☐ Has little to no regard for negative consequences resulting from their words or actions
- ☐ Will violate others' boundaries without regret or remorse
- ☐ Will lose it and throw things, punch holes in the wall, or resort to physical violence

_____

_____

_____

_____ **SEAL Team Force**—A powerful and exacting pattern.
- [ ] Acts like a master drill sergeant
- [ ] Is skilled at controlling, intimidating, and guarding; can be hypervigilant, insecure, or overly secure
- [ ] Has an armory of weapons to use for any offensive actions they compulsively take
- [ ] Turns triggers into battle scenes and all-night arguments
- [ ] Can act like a bulldog with a bone, not letting anything go until they win
- [ ] Relies on escape plans and barks orders to feel in control
- [ ] Tries to intimidate others to accomplish their goals and outcomes

_____

_____

_____

_____ **Addict**—Has a low self-esteem and tends to engage in grandiose thinking as well as impulsive and compulsive behaviors.
- [ ] May seem empty, withdrawn, detached, obsessive-compulsive, spontaneous, or unreliable
- [ ] Makes choices that allow them to numb or run away from discomfort
- [ ] Has trouble handling stress and self-regulating
- [ ] May become disconnected and cautious in relationships
- [ ] May seek adventure and risk-taking activities
- [ ] Uses substances or situations like alcohol, tobacco, drugs, pornography, money, plastic surgery, sex, exercising, shopping,

social media, or gambling to cover up unresolved pain and shame, to resist the truth, or to play it safe and hide

_____

_____

_____

_____ **Bully**—Is a strong pattern that prefers to control and is prone to frustration and feeling annoyed.
- [ ] May be aggressive, domineering, belittling, afraid of vulnerability, or insecure
- [ ] Usually lacks empathy and compassion and is not sympathetic to the needs or desires of others
- [ ] Has little respect for authority
- [ ] Has challenges following rules
- [ ] Blames others for their own bad behavior
- [ ] Picks out others' insecurities and acts out in a superior posture
- [ ] Mistakes others' fear of their oppression and arrogance for admiration and validation

_____

_____

_____

_____ **Witchy Bitchy**—Like the Bully, but meaner and more chaotic.
- [ ] Represents unrestrained (right brain–dominant) patterns
- [ ] Gets upset and hostile in a way that attracts attention and causes suffering
- [ ] Acts belligerently, unreasonably, maliciously, controllingly, aggressively, or dominantly
- [ ] May be extremely emotional or apologetic after bouts of rage or shutdowns but does not know how to control their behavior
- [ ] Has challenges controlling their emotions and seems to lose control of themselves when this pattern is activated

_____

_____

_____

_____ **A$$ Holer**—Like the Bully, but angrier and more unhinged.

- ☐ Represents unrestrained (left brain–dominant) patterns
- ☐ Gets upset and hostile in a way that attracts attention and causes suffering
- ☐ Acts childlike with their anger and destructive verbal and non-verbal patterns
- ☐ Has trouble remembering things and can be extremely emotional, lacking foresight
- ☐ May be extremely emotional or apologetic after bouts of rage or shutdowns but does not know how to control their behavior
- ☐ Has challenges controlling their emotions and seems to lose control of themselves when this pattern is activated

_____

_____

_____

_____ **F*ck You'itis**—The most powerful and destructive of the PODS. It is activated when they perceive a major threat to their inner world.

- ☐ Comes wrapped in explosives and gazes maniacally at a big shiny detonator
- ☐ Says "Ah, f*ck it, I don't give a damn!" in a stressful situation
- ☐ Has a tendency to take others down with them
- ☐ Creates hailstorms of chaos and derails the train from the tracks
- ☐ Clears the Monopoly board when they realize they have lost or throws the remote control when they flip their lid

☐ To protect the NUB, they might destroy their own bodies, relationships, situations, careers, or anything else in their path

_____

_____

_____

Are there any other PODS not listed above that you feel best describe your guardians? Please list and describe them here.

_____

_____

_____

After you rank each PODS, list the top five PODS that challenge you the most in your life below:

1. _____

2. _____

3. _____

4. _____

5. _____

Section 2:
Identify Your PODS' Weapons of Choice

Each PODS has its own array of weapons of choice. Place an *X* to the left of each verb that reflects your PODS' weapons of choice. This is your time to be accountable to yourself and display your new standards of HAVOR (**h**onest, **a**uthentic, **v**ulnerable, **o**pen, and **re**al).

__ Accommodate	__ Accuse	__ Act aloof, cold
__ Analyze	__ Appease	__ Assume
__ Attack	__ Avoid	__ Blame
__ Cajole	__ Chase	__ Clam up
__ Cling	__ Complain	__ Condemn
__ Confront	__ Control	__ Counter
__ Criticize	__ Debate	__ Deceive
__ Defend	__ Deflect	__ Demand
__ Demean	__ Deny	__ Disapprove
__ Dismiss	__ Excuse	__ Gaslight
__ Get quiet	__ Give advice	__ Ignore
__ Interrogate	__ Invalidate	__ Judge
__ Justify	__ Leave	__ Lecture
__ Lie	__ Manipulate	__ Make a point
__ Minimize	__ Mock	__ Nag
__ Not respond	__ Numb out	__ Obsess

___ One-up   ___ Passive-aggressive   ___ Physically act out

___ Pick fights   ___ Placate   ___ Play games

___ Poke   ___ Pout   ___ Preach

___ Put down   ___ Question   ___ Rage

___ Rationalize   ___ Reason   ___ Sass, get sarcastic

___ Scream   ___ Shame   ___ Shut down

___ Stonewall   ___ Throw things   ___ Text, call excessively

___ Use humor   ___ Withdraw   ___ Yell

List any other verbs that describe your weapons of choice as well as how they make you and others feel once they are deployed.

_____

_____

_____

_____

_____

_____

Now, rank your top five weapons of choice below:

1. _____

2. _____

3. _____

4. _____

5. _____

Once you have finished your list, use AI, VAK It Up, and BSI to imagine being a bird overlooking a corn maze that represents the boundary of your Triggered Protective Cycle. Imagine watching yourself in the maze, embroiled in conflict. Describe how your PODS use their weapons of choice through nonverbal signals. Pay close attention to each of the nonverbals below and describe what they look like when your PODS have activated, and you are using their weapons of choice:

- Facial expressions
- Speech patterns
- Body language
- Breathing patterns
- Energy emission

_____

_____

_____

_____

_____

Ask yourself if any of these patterns seem eerily similar, like ones you saw or used in your youth. If so, list the patterns and the people you believe you may have either adapted to or adopted the pattern from.

_____

_____

_____

_____

_____

_____

You may wish to continue revisiting this exercise, as our PODS usually have a lot to say! Take note of any feelings that arise, as working with our PODS is seldom comfortable or easy. However, it is necessary work. Our PODS can wreak havoc, but they are not the enemy; they are simply adaptive roles we have formed to protect ourselves. As you deepen into the process of embodying your MEL over time, the PODS will come to recognize that their tactics are no longer needed and there is a healthier way to operate.

Many of my clients have wrestled with their PODS and wondered, *Why am I the way I am?* This process is not meant to mire you in a pit of judgment or despair. Your awareness will make all the difference so the internal conflict can finally come to an end, and you can experience the freedom and joy of connecting with your MEL most of the time. (Remember, we're all imperfect human beings and shift happens, but we can observe the Law of 80/20: We can strive to be in our MEL 100 percent of the time, but be grateful when we get to 80 percent as we lovingly manage the remaining 20 percent we're still working on.)

CHAPTER 11

Step 2, Part 1: Introduction to SIMEs

The cry we hear from deep in our hearts,
comes from the wounded child within.
Healing this inner child's pain is the key to
transforming anger, sadness, and fear.

—Thich Nhat Hanh

The primary purpose for the Re-Claiming Process is to clear and cleanse your Core Identity Cycle, which is adversely affecting your present-day life. We all have some form of NUBs originating either in childhood or in our adult lives. As I have stated many times, our nervous system is not so much concerned about what happens to us (content) as it is with what happens within us (context).

The essence of the Re-Claiming Process is to learn how to perform neurological surgery on yourself. This amazing journey of self-healing and growth transforms your disempowered patterns and helps resolve conflicts within and with others as you integrate back into wholeness. Remember, your journey is uniquely yours, so I encourage you to regard it with a sense of awe and humility; each of us is truly like a snowflake, and it is pointless to attempt to compare our struggles and triumphs with those of anyone else.

Throughout the process, you will be guided to step into the shoes of the MEL of your inner world. Here, you will encounter your PODS and gain their trust, thereby transforming your relationship with them from one of resistance into one of acceptance so that you have their full permission to perform the procedures. You can certainly do the work even if you don't have their full permission, but it helps a lot when you do. If your PODS don't trust your MEL, you must obtain that trust before proceeding. You then meet your NUBs, who represent your inner children or wounded adults, wherever they are stuck, frozen in time. You will witness them and understand their story, validate their experience, and empathize with their feelings to create a secure attachment bond with all your various aspects. You will guide them to express, process, and integrate back to wholeness. You then install new empowered values and resources to complete the process. When this occurs, you decrease the impact the Core Identity Cycle has on the Triggered Protective Cycle and your PODS.

Strategic Intentional Meditative Experiences (SIMEs)

SIMEs constitute the primary technique we use in the Re-Claiming Process. These are guided meditative journeys designed for inner healing, growth, and manifesting your future. SIMEs are intended to assist your unconscious mind to reveal, release, and resolve cycles that no longer serve you. The Core Identity Cycle resides in the unconscious mind until you bring it into your conscious awareness. The energy and information locked within contain the "virus," the corrupted programming codes that are at the heart of our unresolved memories. The body is the hard drive that stores these unresolved memories, which go on to activate the Core Identity and Triggered Protective Cycles.

Depending on your specific needs and goals, the processes of the SIMEs help achieve three outcomes: The first is to heal you from within and resolve whatever is causing you to suffer and struggle. The second interrupts and replaces present patterns that are causing you and others some form of negativity, obstruction, turmoil, and conflict. The third is for you to design and declare your vision for the future to achieve whatever goals you desire and for you to grow into the next highest version of yourself.

When you understand the power and influence your unconscious mind has on your life, you can then use specialized NI techniques to communicate with it in a way that facilitates clearing and cleansing your past, making mindful changes in the present, or designing and directing your future. The unconscious mind loves to serve and follow clear suggestions. Unfortunately, people often send directives to their unconscious mind that associate with and activate some disempowered pattern from the past. This results in reenacting and reinforcing that pattern and validating and perpetuating those disempowered beliefs.

During a SIME, I make suggestions that involve the three most important sensory inputs: sight, sound, and feelings. SIMEs happen inside you. Most of the time, I never know the details of a person's journey until they share them with me afterward. Remember, it is not so much about what happens to you—the content—but what happens within you—the context. Overall, the various steps of the Re-Claiming Process are a bottom-up approach versus a top-down approach, which is used in many modalities. In other words, we begin with the body and work our way up to the head—we begin with the roots of the tree before we trim the limbs and branches.

There are two ways you can work with a SIME.

1. In the *active process*, you move your body to generate intensity. You physically act out the scene and display the emotion to facilitate increasing the intensity and replicating the nonverbal aspects of the sensory inputs.

2. The *passive process* is a more traditional meditative practice in that you sit in a comfortable position with your eyes closed and create the sensory inputs in your mind's eye. You match your nonverbal signals to the sensory inputs, and you use your breath to increase the intensity of the emotion you're feeling.

One goal for a SIME is to allow your unconscious mind to guide you toward integration. This requires you to differentiate yourself from your PODS and step into your MEL. Then you'll continue the journey to reveal, release, and resolve your vulnerable NUBs. In essence, you are revealing the Core Identity Cycle, releasing the painful emotions and disempowered beliefs, and resolving the cycle so it can no longer be activated so easily. In essence, SIMEs are journeys to cleanse your past, manage your present, and direct your future.

Another goal of a SIME is to release any energy that has not been digested. These are painful emotions stuck in the NUBs that can be one, ten, thirty, or sixty years old. Remember, the unconscious mind has no concept of time or space!

You also use SIMEs to change any viruses that were imprinted into your programming codes. You use the journeys to go back in time and change the red meaning you unconsciously assigned in the past to a new green-empowered meaning in the present.

Overall, when we use a SIME to resolve the past, we are looking to achieve three things:

1. Change the disempowered meaning of an unresolved memory into an empowered meaning.
2. Acquire our life learning lessons from past experiences and bring them into the present.
3. Install MEL values that act as resources for resilience as we move forward.

Although we can't change the content of what happened to us, we can absolutely change the context by changing how we are making sense of the past in the present moment.

An analogy we can use is a strand of pearls. The Core Identity Cycle has two components: meaning and emotion. When we closely identify the first event, the first pearl on the strand, and then cut the string right after the first pearl, what happens to the rest of the pearls? They all fall off. So, when you change the meaning of an experience, the corresponding emotions also transform.

Important Distinctions Before You Move into a SIME

Hippocrates said, "Before you heal someone, ask him if he is willing to give up the things that made him sick."

When we apply this to the Re-Claiming Process, we see that it's important to identify the unhealed aspects that are making our lives difficult. Ultimately, you must compassionately differentiate from and not integrate with your protective patterns. Then, you can go through the multistep process to reveal, release, and resolve your NUBs, which contain your painful emotions and disempowered beliefs. You, as your MEL, will work toward creating a secure attachment bond with your NUBs. Your goal is to decrease reactivity and the negative consequences it has on your inner and outer worlds.

The following distinctions are the practical elements to ingrain before performing your inner-world surgery. I have mentioned some of these distinctions before, but I include them here to help you further embed the foundational applications that ensure your neurological success.

Connect to Your Body

You must discover how to be attentive and become mindful of the changes in your physiology and intentionally engage in strategies to decrease activation. Pay attention to the signals from your body to interrupt reactive patterns, lower your NSI to a 3 or below, and return to a flexible state inside the zone of tolerance. Many people live in their heads and are not attuned to their body's messages; sometimes, even when they are, they don't listen! This is one of the major causes of repeating disempowered choices—people may hear the whispers of wisdom from their MEL but have not learned to trust it and instead stay on autopilot, believing whatever story is playing in their head. When we learn to respect our body as the warehouse of intuition and wisdom, everything about our experience shifts.

Self-Soothe

One of the biggest benefits of going through the Re-Claiming Process is learning how to mindfully use the NI strategies, tools, and techniques to soothe your nervous system. If you are one of the fortunate ones who grew up with an insecure attachment style (like me), you have challenges managing your nervous system. When you were young, you did not learn how to self-soothe and come back into the zone of tolerance. When you acquire the ability to self-regulate your nervous system, you become aware of when you approach the threshold and know how to intentionally flow back into flexibility. You become proficient at using your new skills to recenter your inner world in the face of life's challenges.

Manage Your Mind

A critical element is the skill of managing your chatterbox mind by remaining mindful of your TEA as well as the language you're using. Your mind is multifaceted and has so many stories it can tell—all of which it believes are incredibly fascinating and loaded with truth. You can learn to be mindful and observe your thoughts rather than engage with them. You do not have to be a bulldog chewing on every bone that comes your way. Your mind will run story after story, and it is up to you to skillfully learn how to respond to it. When a thought pops up, you have the choice to observe and not engage with it. You can come back to the present moment with loving kindness to yourself.

A long time ago, I created what I called the twelve apps, acronyms I shared with clients for learning purposes. The fifth app was called Stop Playing GAMES with Yourself. GAMES stands for **g**rab, **a**ttach **m**eaning, and **e**xpunge a **s**tory. We do not have to grab every thought, attach a meaning to it, then narrate the story that goes with it. We have a choice to keep ourselves from getting caught by a disempowered thought!

Quiet Your Mind

A wonderful benefit of doing this work is learning how to quiet your mind, which is all about dropping into a relaxed space that keeps you from engaging with random thoughts. When you are participating in a SIME journey, you allow yourself to go quiet and dark above the eyes. You slow down, allow time to stand still, and relax your body. You learn how to observe but not engage your thoughts. You know your mind is not you and you are not your mind. You appreciate how to differentiate and not integrate with your PODS. You train yourself not to get caught by a thought, and if you do, to come back to the present moment with loving kindness. In essence, you witness yourself without losing yourself.

Suspend Your Critical Faculty

One of the most crucial elements of the Re-Claiming Process is honing the ability to suspend your critical faculty. This is the aspect of you that wants to distinguish between fantasy and reality. Remember back when you were a kid, and you 100 percent believed in Santa Claus or the Tooth Fairy? Then, one day, your prefrontal cortex developed, and the external world helped you differentiate between fact and fiction. When you watch a Marvel movie and see the superheroes battling supervillains, you don't sit there and debate whether Captain America has super-strength or if Thor is a real-life character. You made a conscious choice before starting to watch the movie to willfully suspend your critical faculty so you could enjoy the journey the movie was about to take you on.

This suspension of reality is necessary for participating in the Re-Claiming Process. As I've mentioned, it the most challenging aspect for my left brain–dominant clients. They have a difficult time letting go of the present to explore the unknowns in their past. Remember, the unconscious mind cannot tell the difference between real, remembered, and imagined. The skill of quieting the mind and letting go of the present allows your imagination the freedom to search for your truth. So, for the purpose of this journey (the most exciting journey you'll ever take as a hero exploring the depths of your inner world), give yourself permission to believe in the make-believe.

Accept Suggestions and Directives–Or Not

As we progress through the steps of the Re-Claiming Process, suggestions and directives will be offered. It is your choice to accept or refuse any of them, without judgment. If you stop to judge, then you are thinking—and if you are thinking, you have not let go of the present moment and are evaluating instead of evolving. It is imperative that you accept suggestions effortlessly in order to see, hear, feel, smell, taste, and sense what is occurring.

I share with my clients that they are the artists for the journey we are about to go on. Throughout this journey, I will place a canvas in front of you and provide you with multiple markers of various colors. As I share the suggestions and directives, you paint your picture. You accept the context and paint the content. If I suggest you are riding on a polka-dotted elephant and you draw a striped giraffe, it's the same context but different content. You get to be the one who paints your own unique vision.

It's Always Your Choice

It is your choice to allow your unconscious mind to work for you instead of trying to manage, control, and manipulate your journey. Let go and let be—you must allow your unconscious mind to go wherever it wants to go and do whenever it needs to do. In this way, it can express itself and process any unresolvedness.

Enjoy the Ride

Give yourself permission to let go, slow down, and allow time to stand still. Play along, play all out, and don't hold back. You just might enjoy forgetting who you are, where you are, and when you are during your journeys. As many of my clients have shared, it's a genuine pleasure to go inside and begin the journey to heal one's own inner world. Traveling to the unique and special parts of us that only we know is like entering the Wonderland of our own inner landscape and learning to be delighted by what we find there.

Claim the Grand Prize

During many of the SIMEs, you learn that you can change the meaning you assigned in the past to a more empowered meaning that serves you moving forward. You can obtain your life learning lessons, which act as your pearls of wisdom. In this way, you begin to acquire resources of resilience and affirm your MEL values, which you can embody and bring back to the present.

My hope is that, through this process, you will use all the NI strategies, tools, and techniques from the previous sections of this book when you feel triggered at some point in the future. At that time, you can more immediately, and more mindfully, manage the inflammation that arises.

You may allow your body to soften and release and your mind to go quiet. Let it be, let it open, and let it go, as it is and as it will be, with loving kindness and an open heart, in the present moment and nonjudgmentally. As you do this, remember to listen for the messages that come up for you instead of thinking of the thoughts that come down to you.

Practice Before You Proceed

Sometimes, people ask me about the difference between SIMEs and meditation. Let me begin by saying that SIMEs and meditation are virtually the same thing. The biggest difference is that SIMEs use specific suggestions to guide you through a vivid inner-world experience during which you actively use AI and VAKing tools. While most meditation is about being aware of the thoughts that are entering and exiting the mind, SIMEs hone the attention in a deeper way and activate the senses to respond accordingly.

All SIMEs are self-controlled, and no one can make you do anything you do not want to do. You are always aware and always in control. The premise is that the recipient of the suggestions accepts them without question, judgment, analyzing, logicalizing, or rationalizing—but the way they accept them is up to them!

This acceptance is the biggest obstacle to the success of this process. The person who is on a SIME journey must suspend judgment and give themselves permission to believe in the make-believe. Again, the two most important neurological instruments we use with SIMEs are AI and VAK It Up.

You may have heard of the word *trance* when it comes to suggestions offered in a hypnotherapy session. The common misperception is that suggestions put people into a trance wherein they lose their ability to think for themselves. This is totally false and misleading. A trance allows a person to go into a deep state of relaxation. That's it. It's just a relaxed state during which their conscious mind goes quiet and their unconscious mind is listening for instructions. Of course, I have my own term for this trance state: the *void of nothingness.*

The void of nothingness occurs when you are in a totally relaxed state and nothing in the external world is in your awareness. You allow your brain to become quiet, and you go dark above the eyes. You are totally present in the moment, in a blissful state of nonjudgment without any sense of time and space. You slow down, let go, and allow time to stand still. In the waking state, your brain waves are at a higher frequency of 14–40 Hz per second, referred to as the beta state. As you begin to relax, you lower that activity in the brain into the alpha state, and the brain cycles slow to 7.5–14 Hz per second. The alpha state is extremely relaxed, kind of like the state you get into when you zone out. The next state is theta, where the brain waves slow even further, to 4–7.5 Hz per second. This is what you feel right before you go to sleep.

The goal of SIMEs is to help you to drop into the void of

nothingness so you achieve a lower-alpha to upper-theta range of brain activity to gain better access to your unconscious mind. SIMEs help you to let your unconscious mind see what it wants to see, go where it wants to go, and do what it needs to do. For that to happen, you must suspend disbelief.

I begin each step of the process with an induction—a script in which I make multiple suggestions to help you relax so you easily drop into a void of nothingness before you begin a journey.

Have you ever been to a movie and experienced a shift in your inner world? Did you get inspired and become uplifted with joy? Did you cry, laugh, or get frightened? You know it was just a movie, and you also accepted what you saw to be real! You suspended judgment, allowed yourself to believe in the make-believe, and accepted the visual and auditory suggestions to affect your inner world. Likewise, have you ever listened to a guided meditation? Did you accept the suggestions given during the meditations? SIMEs are very much like guided meditations, which allow you to listen for suggestions and directives; it is up to you to decide whether to accept them or not.

Now, let me demonstrate to you what a SIME feels like. Notice that you are breathing in through your nose and out through your mouth in a natural rhythmic manner, as you inhale deeply and exhale with intention, keeping your body open, allowing energy to flow, and listening for the messages from below. Now, close your eyes, please, for seven seconds, and then open them. That's it. It just feels like that! You will remain aware of everything at all times. It's not all that different from a guided meditation, except for the fact that the journey you're embarking on is highly intentional and strategic, whereas a guided meditation might have a more generalized purpose.

Now, close your eyes as I ask you to place your hands on your thighs. Next, put your feet together on the floor. Now, go into the corner and stand on your head. You agreed to close your eyes, to put your hands on your thighs, and to put your feet together on the floor. However, you weren't about to stand on your head! My point is this: SIMEs simply cannot *make* you do anything. They only make it easy to achieve what you want to achieve. They cannot make you want to do it, either. That's *your* part.

Now, will you willfully suspend judgment, allow yourself to believe in the make-believe, play along, and play all out? I promise that if you do—if you make the determination to connect with your inner world for the purpose of learning, stretching, healing, and growing—the results will be beyond astounding. I know because I've seen it countless times before, even with my clients with left-brainitis.

CHAPTER 12

The Rest of the Steps
of the Re-Claiming Process

In response to threat and injury, animals (including humans) execute biologically based, non-conscious action patterns that prepare them to meet a threat and defend themselves. The very structure of trauma—including activation, dissociation, and freezing— are based on the evolution of survival behaviors. Trauma is hell on earth. Trauma resolved is a gift from the gods.

—Peter A. Levine

From this point onward, I will briefly discuss some of the details for the steps of the Re-Claiming Process. You'll find QR codes for step 2 (parts 1 and 2) and step 3 (parts 1, 2 and 3). The QR codes will take you to the resource page on the Center for Neurological Intelligence website (centerforni.com/resources) where you will find the various meditations and other resources to assist you on your journey. The five SIMEs from steps 2 and 3 are the Introductory Induction (step 2, part 1); the Journey Induction (step 2, part 2); and Associate and Activate Your MEL (part 1—present, part 2—past, and part 3—future).

For the remainder of the steps, I will be offering live workshops in person and online, so that you can get the most out of the Re-Claiming Process. This is absolutely interactive, as we cannot always predict what will happen when we go into the steps. In order to bring this work to you with the highest ethics and greatest responsibility, I made the decision that the remainder of the steps occur in a safe, empowering container that allows you to go deep without getting lost or over-whelmed. You'll be able to find more information about upcoming workshops for steps 4 through 9 of the Re-Claiming Process on my website.

In truth, all the steps of the Re-Claiming Process (even the first five SIMEs) are meant to be interactive, as I will be offering you direc-tives and asking questions throughout, meaning your conscious mind will interact with me by conveying what your unconscious mind is revealing to you. As I lead you on a SIME I may have you write down any answers to questions I pose or ask you to jot down any insights that come up for you. I suggest buddying up with someone you trust so they can record your responses. This way, you can keep your eyes closed and stay in a relaxed state to continue flowing during the process without having to come out of your void of nothingness to record your answers.

Step 2, Part 1:
Practice Induction

Scan the QR code on the next page, which will take you to the first SIME. The Practice Induction is crucial in learning how to participate in a SIME. Chapter 11 led you through the educational aspects of step 2, part 1. The next phase of part 1 is learning and practicing using the timeline technique. This technique will be used often with the rest of the steps. You will take a "test flight" to get acquainted with using it. Next, you will enjoy your first induction to practice, letting go of the present, relaxing your inner world, and utilizing the 4-6-8 intentional breathing technique. The journey will end with your first MEL values installation.

Step 2, Part 2:
A Challenge to Sharpen Your Tools

Scan the QR code below, which will take you to the next SIME. This journey induction is designed to further assist you in letting go of the present so that you will be able to let go of the past. This SIME will challenge you to use your most important neurological instruments: AI and VAK It Up. You will begin with an induction, and then I will make specific suggestions for you to see, hear, feel, and sense. This is your time to learn how to give yourself permission to believe in the make-believe as you enjoy four mini-journeys during this practice SIME to prepare you for the deeper work ahead.

Bonus SIME: On page 310 you'll find a QR code you can scan to take you to a SIME to practice becoming proficient with the neurological instruments.

Step 3:
Associate with and Activate Your MEL

There are three QR codes below, which will take you to the next set of SIMEs. They will allow you to begin to define and refine your higher self. In step 1, part 1, you began to associate and activate the magnificent MEL that lies within. In step 3, you will participate in three SIMEs to further identify and define your MEL in three areas of life.

In step 3.1, you will work in the present to associate with and activate your MEL in various realms of your life, beginning with your relationship to yourself. In step 3.2, you will venture into the past and identify a recent event, situation, or time period in which you felt challenged and got triggered and reactive with yourself or others. In step 3.3, you will go out into the future and begin to use your MEL values to design and attract your desired future.

3.1   3.2   3.3

Step 4:
Exploratory Experiential

Now that you've done the important preparatory work, this will be your first dive within (in the expansive container of one-on-one coaching or a workshop format, during which I can offer more customized guidance and direction). This SIME will be your first journey inside your inner world, which will allow you to discover that which you may be unaware of by revealing your NUBs in greater depth. I will begin with an induction and then make suggestions for you to travel through time and space to a unique destination. You will have the choice to allow your unconscious mind to make explicit that which was implicit. My hope is for you to have an experience during which you discover and uncover that which you allow yourself to fully see, hear, feel, and sense.

Step 5:
Transfer and Transform Energy

In this step, you'll train your mind to tame your body. Let me explain what I mean by this. When you have NUBs that are stuck, frozen in time in your body, you can associate with and activate them. When this occurs, you feel dis-ease and initiate disempowered patterns to hide from, run from, numb, or squash any unresolved painful emotions and uncomfortable body sensations. This step is about working with the residue of a NUB, in the form of the energy in your body, rather than the memory of a specific INE.

This is your first experiential process to transfer out painful emotions and uncomfortable body sensations and transform these into an empowered alternative. You will have a choice to work with one or both of the common unresolved emotional bundles that become stuck in our inner world: the constellation of resentment, contempt, and anger, or that of grief, pain, sadness. This step gives you tools that will enable you to become comfortable with that which was uncomfortable and start to create a secure attachment for yourself.

Step 6:
Meet and Greet Your PODS . . . As Your MEL!

In step 6, you'll create secure attachments with your inner guardians. I hope you put in the time and effort to complete the exercise in step 1, part 3 (chapter 10). At the conclusion, you came up with your top five PODS, which will be the ones you will work with during this step. Now, it is time to reconnect with them as your magnificent MEL. You will get to know your PODS and work through various phases to connect and construct a secure attachment bond with these aspects of self. Remember, you're not trying to eliminate your PODS. Instead, you are compassionately but firmly allowing your MEL to take the lead. It is important to differentiate and not integrate with your PODS to separate (with love, acceptance, and compassion) from any red patterns that are ruling you. When you integrate with your PODS, you get mesmerized by the cacophony of commentators chattering their various disempowered stories rather than listening to the wisdom and intuition of your MEL. It is critical to stay present, nonjudgmental, centered, and grounded as your MEL. This is how the PODS begin to establish a sense of safety, certainty, and trust. Your MEL must become their ally and not their adversary.

Step 7:
NUB Hunting

This is the step that will allow you to scan for what may remain unresolved, as you might end up unearthing a NUB that you didn't know was there. You will scan your timeline and allow your unconscious mind to direct you to locate any unresolved NUBs that may be stuck, frozen in time.

Please know that this step is not about reliving any INEs that are unresolved or retraumatizing yourself. You'll be focused on discovering the composition (the painful emotions and disempowered beliefs) of the NUB, its global story, and concise information regarding when and how it fractured and formed. This is a quick process to locate anything that's unresolved; and if you discover any unresolved NUBs, you'll explore these in step 8.

Step 8:
Reveal, Release, and Resolve SIMEs

The SIMEs of step 8 are the heart and soul of the Re-Claiming Process where all the prep work you have done comes together. You will use all the neurological instruments and VAKing tools at your disposal for this all-inclusive journey. Step 8 has the potential to be your profoundest healing experience if you trust and allow your unconscious mind to do what it wants and needs to do.

There are many variations to this multifaceted journey, and it has numerous intentions. The primary purpose is the work to reveal, release, and resolve your vulnerable NUBs and transform your PODS to reclaim your wholeness. Some other examples are situational experiences based on what you might be going through, such as letting go of energetic bonds, releasing past lovers, or connecting with the spiritual aspects of loved ones who have passed away.

The SIMEs of step 8 are unique to the person experiencing it in a one-on-one coaching environment. In the workshops and webinars I lead, I take people through several variations of SIMEs so they can finish the process of conducting neurological surgery on themselves.

This is experiential healing from the inside out. Here's the best part: I don't need to know the details of the memory my clients are working on; I just need enough information to guide them through the process. Assuming you are working on a NUB, then I need to know the approximate age; body location where it's stuck, frozen in time; the antagonist(s) associated with the INE; and the PODS that have come along to witness this process. That's it!

When working with NUBs, there are many ways to structure the journey depending on your needs and what would work best for your unique experience. In my one-on-one coaching and workshops, I will offer you the chance to determine the various destinations where you will choose to go. The greatest gift you can give yourself is to reveal, release, and resolve the unresolved and come back home to your original innate wholeness.

Step 9:
The Big Sweep

Step 9 is an energetic SIME that clears and cleanses your timeline; it's like taking a giant broom and sweeping away any leftover crumbs after you have completed step 8. You will use a timeline experiential to locate any leftover painful emotions and disempowered beliefs. You will go back in time to finish clearing and cleansing any residual neurological wounds. Remember, no process is one and done. We must always double-check to show our unconscious mind our new, mindful, empowered reality.

Conclusion

Until you are willing to be confused about what you already know, what you know will never grow bigger, better, or more useful.

–Milton H. Erickson

Congratulations! I acknowledge and applaud you for getting to the end of volume 2. I hope you worked through all the exercises to go deep inside your inner world so you can start to become proficient with the NI strategies, tools, and techniques that you feel resonate the most and work best for you.

I always share with clients that I can guide them along their journey. Together, we learn, explore, and practice in our sessions, but the degree of their success is dependent not on our time together but on their dedication and commitment to applying the tools in their NI toolbox from moment to moment. The real challenge for my clients is to become flexible and give themselves permission to stop arguing for their limitations and simply allow some of their disempowered stories to be inaccurate, incomplete, or incorrect. They need to take the time to learn and practice the neurological instruments and anchors of awareness and to trust and allow the instruments of AI and VAK It Up to work for them, using intentional, consciously driven, massive sensory data to give themselves the greatest chance of success.

Recall from volume 1 that you must become consciously competent to engage a pattern long enough with mindful repetition before you train your unconscious mind to become unconsciously competent. At this point, employing new, empowered patterns will occur automatically. Over time, you will alter your autopilot programming by flipping your references from red to green. The question is, which patterns serve you and which cause you and others to suffer?

One of the greatest gifts we can give ourselves when shift happens in our inner world is to exercise awareness and take ownership, without self-judgment, of our reactive traits, states, and patterns. (And believe me, we all have them!) You have a wonderful opportunity here—and it has nothing to do with becoming perfect (remember, there's no such thing). It's about learning to embrace and love all aspects of who you are, including your NUBs, PODS, and your uniquely special brand of weirdness. All that's required is the practice of slowing down, quieting your mind, going downstairs, and learning how to trust and listen to the wisdom and intuition coming from down below. Over time, the work of NI will help you practice associating with and activating your MEL to bring forth the values you'll need, from moment to moment, to lean into your resistance—and then to make a responsive choice to step into the space of discomfort and notice your reactive body sensations. You can use all the NI strategies, tools, and techniques in this book to begin interrupting your reactive patterns; you can learn to be courageous and patient as you become increasingly comfortable with that which used to be uncomfortable and to lower your NSI below a 3.

I gain so much pleasure when I work with clients who have proven to themselves that they can do the work of managing their inner world. I have worked with so many people who have made breakthroughs in how they see themselves and the world around them—all because they have discovered that change truly is possible, and it begins within. We can take the steps toward transforming the meaning we've placed on an experience or situation; we can honor and love our BETTY and step into HAVOR. When I see clients lovingly proving to themselves that healing is possible, and that it begins with the choices they make,

I experience such a sense of joy and validation. I know that NI works, and it is deeply gratifying to watch people in the process of making it work for themselves.

To learn, stretch, heal, grow, and update your human operating system, you must do so from the inside out. You must *win from within* to heal whatever remains unresolved, reclaim your inner world, and grow into the next highest version of yourself. This may sound abstract, but it isn't. This book has given you the necessary information (which is yours to experience firsthand) to live with a quiet mind, a loving heart, a peaceful soul, and a calm body—and to enjoy happy, healthy, harmonious relationships with others and with yourself. The process will require you to dive deep and be bold when it comes to exploring your vast inner terrain. Think of this book as a blueprint offering infinite ways to work with the NI strategies, tools, and techniques. Find what works best for you. As the famous saying goes, "Plan your work and work your plan."

Remember that every single one of us is programmed by sensory data from the time we were born all the way to the present moment. Now, you have the knowledge that's necessary for you to start mindfully manufacturing massive amounts of sensory data so that you can interrupt disempowered patterns and fulfill your goals and dreams. Healing is not a passive process of waiting for the "right moment" or for some distant future in which you will be magically improved. It is a process of engaging both your conscious choices and unconscious mind as you step into your MEL and lovingly shift the harmful patterns that are holding you back from your next highest version of self.

So many of us are terrified of change because we don't know what lies on the other side. But with the supportive guidance of your MEL, you can navigate anything that comes your way. You can practice the NI strategies, tools, and techniques in this book right in the moment of conflict so that you can continue to embody your MEL and lovingly engage with your life as you regulate your nervous system and stay below a NSI 3.

Everything you've read here applies to your relationship with yourself and with anyone else in your life. If you are in a committed love relationship or desire to be in one, I invite you to continue your journey of gaining Neurological Intelligence with volume 3, which focuses on how to apply everything you've learned to create, obtain, and sustain an empowered loving relationship. Imagine how different the world would be if more of us were in secure attachment bonds wherein we could lovingly express the full scope of who we are!

It has been my honor to present to you the culmination of my life's work. I hope to meet you in person or online to guide you on your journey to learning, stretching, healing, and growing so that you can continue to grow into the person you were always meant to be.

Language of NI:
Key Terms and Definitions

4-6-8 Intentional Breathing Technique: You begin by taking a deep inhalation for *four seconds*. Next, you hold your breath for *six seconds* before slowly exhaling, with intention, for *eight seconds*. I suggest you make an audible sigh of relief when you are exhaling, which allows more energy to move through your vocal cords. Repeat this technique five times and witness how it quiets your mind and calms your body.

AEOs (Agendas, Expectations, Obligations): AEOs act as rules we create to validate a belief associated to a value, like fairness or loyalty. We assign AEOs for what needs to happen or not happen for a belief to be true or false. Rules come in two forms: green-empowered (boundaries for what we will and will not accept) and red-disempowered (trying to control someone or something external of self).

AI (Active Imagination): You use active imagination to consciously communicate with your unconscious mind, using your conscious mind to willfully suspend disbelief and choose to believe in the make-believe. You give yourself permission to disregard your left brain's craving to think, judge, analyze, logicalize, rationalize, strategize, and figure out everything.

Anchors of Awareness: Anchors of awareness consist of mindfulness strategies and VAKing tools. When you get triggered, you will feel a stimulus in your body. In order to begin the process of recognizing and interrupting an activated disempowered pattern, you need to apply the anchors of awareness to be cognizant that your body is sending you a signal for your conscious mind to wake up and pay attention.

Awareness, Understanding, Application: First, you become *aware* of any disempowered cycles that are negatively impacting your life and relationships. Second, you come to *understand* how to use NI strategies and tools to recognize and interrupt them and techniques to install new empowered cycles through repetition. Next and most importantly, you *apply* the NI strategies, tools, and techniques by making a conscious commitment to do the daily work necessary to ensure your greatest chance of success.

Beliefs: The mental models we construct, based on real or imagined perceptions of experiences we have with respect to ourselves and others. Beliefs are formed from decisions we make when a reference and a meaning have been repeatedly associated with in times of peak elevated emotions. Beliefs can motivate us to grow and contribute in powerful ways, but they can also act like a mushroom cap—a safe, covered space to keep us from growing and achieving.

BETTY (Be Enthusiastically True to You): When you do not love and honor BETTY, you give your personal power away. When you give your power away, you do not see the truth or listen to the wisdom of your inner voice. When you do not listen to your inner voice, you make decisions that are not aligned with your MEL values. When you are not honoring your MEL values, you are not being true to you, your mind cannot become quiet, and your soul cannot be at peace.

BSI (Body Sensation Impression): The visual representation of a NUB or PODS. The unconscious mind loves symbols, so we use active imagination and sensory data to paint a metaphorical picture of the body sensation. To do that, we describe the location, size, shape, color, temperature, texture, weight, pressure, vibration, etc.

Challenge Question: *What would I have to believe in order to feel this way?* What would you have to believe about the situation, thought, person, place, or thing that triggered you and manifested the physiological shift of emotional energy and body sensation in order for you to feel the way you felt at that time?

Chaos: A reactive state of being hyperaroused and likely to act out or move against others. You usually shout out, and your thoughts might seem like they are racing at 1,000 mph. Some patterns associated with this state are hyperactivity, anxiety, panic, restlessness, insomnia, hypervigilance, hostility, rage, emotional flooding, high blood pressure, and digestive issues.

Conscious Mind: Contains everything within our present awareness. We are consciously aware of approximately 10 percent of what is going on at any moment. When we focus on the present, our conscious mind is aware, just as it is when we daydream or retrieve a past memory. We use our conscious mind to set goals for what we want to achieve and send instructions to our unconscious mind.

Core Identity Cycle: The neurological cycle that begins in childhood with the filtering of sensory data through references generated by past experiences. References are neural pathways that formed when we made sense of an experience; they are context-related and can be positive or negative. References lead us to assign a meaning with an associated emotion, and this can lead us to construct a belief that then becomes a part of our identity. We may not even consciously know where a belief comes from, or which memory it's associated with, but that doesn't stop it from leading us to unconsciously reenact and reinforce disempowering patterns throughout various stages of our lives.

DABA (Denial, Accusation, Blaming, Assuming): When a red-disempowered AEO rule is broken, we may feel pain. We are our own supreme court justice, so we pass down verdicts. We may *deny* we have anything to do with the problem, *accuse* and *blame* others, and *assume* others' thoughts, feelings, and intentions without asking. We adopt a victim story based on the red AEO rule and begin to punish our perceived offender.

Disempowerment: Represented by the color red. In a disempowered state, you resist taking personal responsibility for your inner world and your patterns of negative thoughts, emotions, behaviors, and stories (TEBS). You live "at effect," meaning you blame someone or something external to you for the state of your inner world— your nervous system. You give your personal power away, adopt a victim role, and believe you have no choice. You may focus on what you *do not* want and get your needs of significance and connection met in an unhealthy manner. Your thoughts are I-centric, and generally, your emotions are anger, sadness, fear, shame, guilt, or hurt. You may have an unconscious habit of using disempowered keywords and phrases in the narrative of your perception.

Dreaded *D*'s: When we are in a reactive state, we are inclined to dance with the dreaded *D*'s: debate, defend, deflect, deny, and dismiss. We make it about the "I" instead of "WE" and seek to be understood before understanding, which can cause a rupture in the relationship with self and others.

Empowerment: Represented by the color green. Empowerment is a continuous process of enhancing personal power by mindfully managing your mind. This state of being is also represented by living with the perspective that you are "at cause," meaning you take personal responsibility for your inner world and your patterns of thoughts, emotions, behaviors, and stories (TEBS). Living with the intentions of empowerment, you strive to honor your most important values. You do not give your personal power away to anyone or anything external to you because you know you are a participant and you have choice. You intentionally focus on what you want and are mindful of getting your attachment needs of significance and connection met in a healthy manner. Your primary thoughts concern the greater good, and your emotions are generally positive and infused with love, joy, peace, passion, excitement, empathy, and gratitude.

EWAS (Early Warning Alarm Signal): A metaphorical image you use to act as your wake-up call to get your prefrontal cortex (your mindful brain) to pay attention and take control. EWAS is when your nervous system associates and activates to unresolvedness within, and you feel a unique body sensation. This sensation is usually felt between the throat and groin. This body sensation is the first indication that you are activated and is used as an anchor of awareness to awaken your conscious mind. You can then employ NI strategies, tools, and techniques to interrupt a disempowered pattern and reevaluate the meaning you assigned to your perception.

FID (Frequency, Intensity, Duration): Frequency (how often you go above an NSI 6 within a consistent context); intensity (how you rate the activation of your nervous system from a 0 to 10); duration (how long your nervous system remains in a state of high activation: A few seconds? A few minutes? An entire day? A week? A year? A lifetime?).

HAVOR (Honest, Authentic, Vulnerable, Open, Real): A standard of being for how you show up for yourself and others, honoring your MEL values consistently and congruently.

INE (Impactful Neurological Experience): Negative experiences where we perceive some form of real or imagined danger that activates our nervous system to a high level for a period of time. INEs occur inside of us and are not always visible to others. When an INE overly activates our nervous system, we may fire and wire in the energy and information of the experience into an unresolved lasting memory (neurological wounding).

JERC (Justifying, Excusing, Rationalizing, Cajoling): The third step of the judgment pattern within the Triggered Protective Cycle. Once a red AEO rule is broken, you pass a DABA verdict and then you *justify*, *excuse*, *rationalize*, and *cajole* to defend your disempowered story to prove you are right to validate your identity.

KISS Method (Keep it Simple, Schmegegge): The KISS method is to remind one to try not to "out-think" the process and to keep the process as simple as possible.

M3 Strategy: M3 lets you decide to use your time, energy, and attention with patience, practice, and perseverance to mindfully manufacture a MEL mini movie with massive amounts of sensory data; as you do so, you'll be using the NI instruments. Depending on the context of the intention for your particular strategy, you need to use the tools three times a day for thirty-three consecutive days. This MEL mini movie can last for three seconds, thiry-three seconds, or three minutes, depending on what you are trying to master.

MEL (Mindful Empowered Leader): The highest version of self, which lives by and honors your most important values. When you identify with and live as your MEL, you manage your nervous system from a perspective of personal empowerment. This leads you to enjoy successful, healthy, functional relationships with yourself and others.

MIND (Meaning-Influenced Narrative Dialogue): A process for how we assign *meaning* to our perceptions, which can *influence* the linguistic *narrative* of the *dialogue* in our mind—whether true, false, or questionable.

Mirror Neurons: A mechanism (like a radar) for receiving vibrational signals that help you understand others' conscious and unconscious intentions.

M&M Technique (Monitor and Modify Reactive Patterns): A multistep strategy you use within the gap to ensure you widen it enough to where you are responsive to make choices that lead you to take the high road of empowerment instead of reacting and making choices that hijack you and take you down the low road of disempowerment.

Neurological Conundrum: When you may find yourself stuck at the bottom or living a Slinky Life where you make some progress and then revert back to where you began.

Neurological Cycles: The four cycles that make up the Re-Claiming Journey: sensory perception, core identity, associate & activate, and triggered protective.

Neurological Detox: An uncomfortable time period of breaking your addictive patterns by being mindful to not grab any hooks or attach a disempowered meaning. In a detox, you expunge the same old red story you have been telling yourself. If you grab the hook, you are feeding your PODS superfood and validating their purpose. The energy associated with a Triggered Protective Cycle activates the body and releases neurotransmitters like epinephrine and adrenaline, causing some people to become addicted to this activated state. It makes people feel energized and alive, even if it causes them and others to suffer.

Neurological Growth Factor: The conditions and situations at the proverbial bottom that can give a person the drive, inspiration, and motivation to begin a healing and growth phase. This is when one may make the choice to change their meaning from red to green, acquire their life lessons, and resource mindful empowered values for resilience.

Neurological Growth Questions: When you ask "What now?" you evaluate the following three variables and focus on the solution, not the problem.
- Meaning: What was the red-disempowered meaning I assigned? What green-empowered meaning can I choose to reframe the meaning so this serves to inspire me to move forward and focus on what I do want in order to grow into the next highest version of myself?
- Learnings: What life lessons am I supposed to acquire from this living laboratory of experience that is trying to teach me something? What are the pearls of wisdom and knowledge I can gain from this experience?
- Values: What are the MEL values I need to resource to become more resilient? What values did I need at that time but did not have access to that I can focus on resourcing so I will be prepared to mindfully employ my strategies and tools?

Neurological Instruments: Eleven foundational processes you will apply to give yourself the greatest chance of success to achieve your goals. The best feature about these instruments is they are all readily accessible and they are all *free to use*.

Neuroplasticity: The ability of neural networks in the brain to change through growth, learning, and reorganization.

NI (Neurological Intelligence): The knowledge of our neural networks and the impact they have on our inner and outer worlds. An understanding of the knowledge and functioning of our nervous system, how our neural networks are formed and programmed, why the nervous system operates on repeating disempowered patterns, and the impact these have on our inner and outer world. Neurological Intelligence encompasses the Re-Claiming Journey and the Re-Claiming Process.

Nonverbal: Signals that include our speech patterns, facial expressions, body language, breathing patterns, and energy emissions via our mirror neurons. Our nonverbals account for 93 percent of how someone makes sense of our communication and how we make sense of others. The remaining 7 percent are the actual words we use.

NSI (Nervous System Index): A way to evaluate your nervous system activation and communicate that condition to yourself or someone else. It is a scale of 0 to 10, where 0 is the lowest level of activation, and 10 represents the highest level. Altogether, the NSI measures emotions, body sensations, and language.

NUB (Neurological Unresolved Bundle): An unresolved bundle of energy and information that contains painful emotions and disempowered beliefs. These are your inner children and wounded adults who are stuck, frozen in time within your inner world. Often, it will seem as if they have risen out of the blue; but in truth, they have been activated and triggered by some internal or external experience—or rather, your perception of that experience.

PODS (Personalities of Offensive and Defensive Strategies): The roles and personae we create in childhood and adulthood to protect a vulnerable aspect of self. These are positive protective patterns we form to guard our NUBs from being triggered and reexperiencing the original pain and disempowered beliefs. Unfortunately, while PODS may have served as wonderful coping mechanisms in the past, they can often unnecessarily sabotage us and keep us from experiencing the full joy, love, inner peace, and quiet mind we long to have.

Poking Holes: The mindful process of applying the strategies and tools to recognize and interrupt disempowered patterns and bust the boundaries of a Triggered Protective Cycle.

Primal Attachment Needs: Safety, certainty, and trust are our primal attachment needs, the basis for how our nervous system evaluates whether or not we are in danger. Connection and significance are the secondary needs that become more pronounced in our personal and committed love relationships.

Primary Attachment Question: *Are you there for me, the way I need you, when I need you the most?* The unconscious mind asks someone of significance this question to assess whether their primal attachment needs of safety, certainty, and trust are fulfilled.

Re-Claiming Journey: The science and educational aspect of Neurological Intelligence.

Re-Claiming Process: The strategies, tools, techniques, and experiential aspect of Neurological Intelligence.

References: Judgments formed from how you made sense of things that are based on meanings, emotions, values, decisions, and beliefs that contain simple words. This begins the formation of meaning, either positive or negative, and is context related. Examples include safe or dangerous, positive or negative, success or failure, pleasure or pain, abundance or scarcity, beginning or end, worthiness or unworthiness, hope or hopelessness.

Rigid: A reactive state of being hypoaroused and likely to shut down or move away from others. You usually withdraw, and your thoughts might be foggy and vague. Some patterns associated with this state are depression, flat affect, lethargy, exhaustion, chronic fatigue, disconnection, disassociation, low blood pressure, and poor digestion.

Sensory Data: Encompasses the energy and information derived from sights, sounds, smells, tastes, touches, and mirror neurons.

SIME (Strategic Intentional Meditative Experience): A guided meditative journey designed for inner healing, growth, and manifesting your future. SIMEs are intended to assist your unconscious mind to reveal, release, and resolve cycles that no longer serve you.

TEA (Time, Energy, Attention): TEA is how you can show up to facilitate changes in your patterns. When you consciously choose to drink empowered green TEA, you use your *time* wisely, manage your *energy* mindfully, and pay *attention* to your focus in ways that bring you what you want. When you consciously or unconsciously choose to drink disempowered red TEA, you end up not mindfully managing your *time*, wasting your *energy*, and focusing your *attention* on what you do not want.

TEBS (Thoughts, Emotions, Behaviors, Stories): These make up the pillars of your patterns, whether positive, neutral, or negative. Your patterns are either green-empowered and serving you or red-disempowered and causing you to suffer.

TFQ (True, False, or Questionable) Filter: A way to evaluate whether the challenge question is true, false, or questionable. Rarely is it true—and if it is, then it is what it is! If it's questionable, place it in your toaster oven or on a shelf in the back of your mind and wait for it to go *bing!* and bring the answer up for you. The vast majority of the time, you will answer false if you are being real and honest with yourself.

Triggered Protective Cycle: This cycle is activated by a perception of the present and fueled by an unresolved Core Identity Cycle formed in the past. This will trigger us to become reactive and initiate patterns of chaos or rigidity. We then engage in disempowered protective patterns that may wreak havoc on the relationships we have with self and others.

Unconscious Mind: The aspect of the mind that we are not conscious of in the present moment. It has no concept of linear time and space and cannot tell the difference between real, remembered, and imagined.

VAK (Visual, Auditory, and Kinesthetic) It Up: You use sensory data to recognize, interrupt, and install new patterns. When you actively imagine a scene, you fill it with vibrant colors, clear sounds, and an awareness of emotions, feelings, and body sensations.

QR Code Resources

Language of NI

MEL Values

Practice Using Neurological Instruments

Bonus SIME

A short SIME designed for you to practice giving yourself permission to let go of the present and allow your mind to go quiet. You will enjoy an induction to relax your inner world, and end with a MEL values installation.

About the Author

Renowned Master Neurological Life Coach Glenn S. Cohen has coached thousands of individuals and couples to reveal, release, and resolve neurological wounding in order to heal and grow into the next highest version of self and create safe, loving, and empowered relationships.

Glenn studied at the University of Texas, graduating with a B.S. in Pharmacy. Since 2003, Glenn has been on an inspired mission to study the hows and whys of human experience—a journey that became his own personal PhD. Glenn read books, listened to experts, and attended workshops, retreats, and trainings that spanned various modalities from the inner child to codependency, trauma, EMDR, interpersonal neurobiology, neuroscience, attachment theory, Emotion-Focused Therapy, Neuro-Linguistic Programming, hypnosis, meditation, mindfulness, Somatic Experiencing, and Internal Family Systems.

Before becoming a Neurological Intelligence life coach, published author, and speaker, Glenn lived through many painful experiences—ones that molded him into an extraordinarily intuitive and insightful coach who truly relates to others' stories of heartaches, challenges, and traumas. This led to the development of his own modality of Neurological Intelligence (NI) to represent the knowledge and functioning of our neural networks and the impact they have on our inner and outer worlds.

Glenn takes his clients—and will take you, the reader—through life-changing growth as he shares the knowledge, strategies, tools,

NEUROLOGICAL INTELLIGENCE

and techniques of NI that enable everyone the choice to repro-gram their inner world and follow the path of self-discovery to live an empowered life of meaning. Glenn lives in Charleston, South Carolina, and works with clients across the country. You may find additional resources and social media links at the Center for Neurological Intelligence at www.centerforni.com.